Season It
WITH
Fun!

*To the many staff members who make working
in a school a fun and rewarding experience.*

Season It
WITH
Fun!

A Year of Recognition, Fun, and Celebrations to Enliven Your School

Diane Hodges

CORWIN
A SAGE Company

For information:

Corwin
A SAGE Company
2455 Teller Road
Thousand Oaks, California 91320
(800) 233-9936
Fax: (800) 417-2466
www.corwin.com

SAGE Ltd.
1 Oliver's Yard
55 City Road
London EC1Y 1SP
United Kingdom

SAGE India Pvt. Ltd.
B 1/I 1 Mohan Cooperative
    Industrial Area
Mathura Road, New Delhi 110 044
India

SAGE Asia-Pacific Pte. Ltd.
33 Pekin Street #02-01
Far East Square
Singapore 048763

Printed in the United States of America

Library of Congress Cataloging-in-Publication Data

Hodges, Diane.
Season it with fun!: a year of recognition, fun, and celebrations to enliven your school/ Diane Hodges.
    p. cm.
Includes bibliographical references and index.
ISBN 978-1-4129-6908-6 (pbk.)
   1. Schools—Exercises and recreations. 2. School improvement programs.
3. Motivation in education. I. Title.

LB3031.H63 2010
371.8′9—dc22   2009043850

This book is printed on acid-free paper.

10   11   12   13   14   10   9   8   7   6   5   4   3   2   1

Acquisitions Editor:	Arnis Burvikovs
Associate Editor:	Desirée A. Bartlett
Production Editor:	Cassandra Margaret Seibel
Copy Editor:	Jenifer Dill
Typesetter:	C&M Digitals (P) Ltd.
Proofreader:	Sarah J. Duffy
Cover Designer:	Rose Storey
Graphic Designer:	Anthony Paular

Contents

Acknowledgments

Thank you to the many contributors, named and unnamed, who shared ideas that were used successfully in their schools. This book is all about you!

As always, a huge *thanks* goes to my very good friend, John Speeter. He has been creating cartoons for my publications for decades, and he keeps me smiling and laughing through all phases of life.

In addition to the fabulous team of professionals at Corwin, I had two women who supported me in this effort. Patricia Maas created and managed the graphic files, and Laurie Gibson of Word Association performed the initial edits. It was such a joy to work with them.

I would also like to thank Eric Baylin. Eric has been a teacher for over 40 years and keeps his colleagues at the Packer Collegiate Institute in Brooklyn, New York, motivated and inspired through creative song writing. I am privileged that he allowed me to use three of his works in this document.

And I want to thank my husband, Gerry, who is looking forward to having his wife back now that the book is done.

—D

About the Author

Diane Hodges is the managing partner of Threshold Group, an educational consulting firm in San Diego. After 30+ years as an educator, she is sharing her insights through books and international speaking events. Her wit and humor have delighted audiences and readers everywhere. She served as an executive director of career and technical education, director of instructional services, director of human resources, secondary principal, counselor, and instructor. She earned her doctorate from Michigan State University, has received 12 national and state awards, and is a bestselling author of eight books.

About the Illustrator

John Speeter began drawing cartoons and illustrations while attending Michigan State University. His drawings have been published nationally in books, newsletters, and periodicals, as well as on the Web. John's creativity extends beyond his artistic abilities: he is also an accomplished musician who plays numerous string instruments and performs in a bluegrass group that appears throughout the Midwest. In addition, he is a healthcare operations executive in Michigan.

CHAPTER 1

Creating a Fun, Rewarding School Climate

An essential element for successful schools is a fun, rewarding climate. Think about where you do your best work. Is it in a place where your efforts are recognized and you feel appreciated? Do you have fun when you are there? Recognition, appreciation, fun, laughter, collegial sharing, celebrations—these contribute to the quality of our lives and to those of the people around us. On the other hand, how many of you are sick of all the recognition you receive at work? How many of you say, "I wish my boss would quit telling me what a great job I am doing so I can actually get some work done" or "If those parents would just quit calling me every day to tell me how much I am appreciated . . . "?

You probably don't experience that enough.

"You can dream, create, design, and build the most wonderful place in the world," Walt Disney said, "but it requires people to make the dream a reality." A school's most valuable resource leaves each night and returns the next morning. A district can have the newest state-of-the-art facility and the best curriculum, but if it doesn't have motivated staff members to meet the students' educational needs, then those assets don't mean anything.

Careers have a cycle. For those of us in education, it typically began in college when we majored in subject areas, took our methods courses, worked as an intern-teacher, and so on. Then we received our first job offer. Think back to that moment. Remember the excitement you felt? Who was the first person you called? Do you remember how thrilled you were that you were going to actually *be* an educator and make a difference in the lives of your students? Do you remember how energized and motivated you were?

> Men and women want to do a good job, a creative job, and if they are provided the proper environment, they will do so.
>
> *—Bell Hewlett*

Shortly after we began those first jobs, we discovered that we hadn't learned all of the skills necessary for success. We then got some on-the-job training, sought coaching from mentors and principals, and developed new skills. As we gained competencies, we also gained confidence. This combination put us in the career cycle of being *enthusiastic* and *growing*. Wouldn't it be great if we spent our entire careers being enthusiastic and growing—if we loved what we were doing so much that we greeted each day with energy and a positive attitude and we continued to try new things and to make an effort to become better every day?

At some point, everyone experiences *career frustrations*. Have you been there yet? If not, you will get there eventually. Your enthusiasm, and perhaps your energy, will diminish. The goal in this situation is to get back to being enthusiastic and growing. However, people can sometimes move into a stage of being *stable* and *stagnant*. Being stable might be OK for a while because you are at least maintaining the status quo, but stagnating is not good. Look around your school. You can probably identify which staff members are in that stage of the career cycle. They are the ones who are unwilling to try anything new or serve on a committee.

When an unmotivated staff member is not using his or her full potential, consider that person's supervisor. Has the supervisor helped the staff member reach his or her full potential in the job? It is incumbent upon the supervisor to establish or allow a supportive environment where people can be their best. If someone is not enthusiastic about work, it is the supervisor's responsibility to find out why and to determine how to best help that person regain his or her lost enthusiasm. If someone has reached the career frustration stage, how do you get that person (or you) back to being enthusiastic and growing? First, you have to ask if it is an achievable goal. I used to tell my staff, "If you can't whistle on your way to work, you don't belong in that job." And I believe that not all educators should be in education. We need to help them into other careers, grade levels, job assignments—whatever it takes to get them whistling on their way to work. It is important to ask, one on one, "What do you like doing? What lights your fire?" If the person is feeling burned out, then he or she must have been lit up at some time. What did that look like? What was the person doing? During this career development process, it is important that the person understands that the lack of enthusiasm might be caused by a mismatch between his or her skills and the job requirements, or a mismatch of personality types with the supervisor or coworkers—all of which could be resolved by a different setting or career area.

> There's a big difference between getting people to come to work and getting them to do their best.
>
> —*Bob Nelson*

RECOGNITION AND APPRECIATION

What keeps educators excited and motivated? Two basic ingredients are *recognition* and *appreciation* from colleagues, administrators, parents, students, and the community for a job well done. People want to be excited about what they do. No one gets up in the morning and says, "I think I will just be mediocre today." People want to do a good job and, given the proper environment and encouragement, they will. Likewise, no one gets up in the morning and says, "I am going to do a great job today—I have dental insurance!" Although important, the strongest motivators are not monetary rewards or benefits. People want to be appreciated for what they do. And when their supervisor and colleagues give recognition and appreciation on their behalf, people do their best.

Currently, there are 3.2 million teachers working in U.S. public schools. It is estimated that by the year 2015, a total of 2.8 million new teachers will need to be hired. Given this, recruiting and retaining good staff members is going to become increasingly important.

> Most of us would rather be ruined by praise than saved by criticism.
>
> —*Norman Vincent Peale*

"I hope it's not too much of an inconvenience for you, but I'm desperate to hold on to our good teachers."

© Aaron Bacall

Unfortunately, the teaching profession has a high turnover rate. An estimated 30% of new teachers quit the profession within the first three years (*Time,* February 25, 2008). It has become increasingly difficult for teachers to support their families with just their salaries. Also, in teaching, there is little motivation for excellence; people who are in education do not receive profit-sharing, bonuses, promotions, and so on, which are motivators and rewards in other career fields. The career ladder for a teacher is a very short one: a teacher reaches the top of the career ladder the first day he or she enters the classroom. That's why recognition and appreciation become important motivators.

Let's clarify the difference between *compensation* and *recognition*—these two items are very different. Some people will say that staff members are recognized every other week—it's called a paycheck. Wrong! That's *compensation.* Compensation is what employees receive for a job assigned to them; it's financial remuneration. Recognition is what employees receive for efforts above and beyond what the job requires of them. "Compensation is a right," says management consultant Rosabeth Moss Kanter. "Recognition is a gift."

> People will forget what you said.
>
> People will forget what you did.
>
> But people will not forget how you made them feel.
>
> —*Unknown*

Formal and Informal Recognition

Recognition can be given in two ways—*formally* and *informally. Formal* awards are predetermined ones given for achievement. It is important to determine what behaviors you want to reward during the year.

> Leaders . . . send *very* clear signals about what's important!
>
> —*Tom Peters*

Some behaviors you may want to reward include the following:

- Attendance
- Years of service
- Student achievement
- Community/school relations
- Parent participation
- Submitting student grades on time
- Helping colleagues
- Mentoring new staff members
- Demonstrating a positive attitude
- Trying new things
- Taking a leadership role
- Teamwork
- Safety

- Giving suggestions for improvement
- Professional development outside of school
- Heroism

> We are what we repeatedly do. Excellence, then, is not an act, but a habit.
>
> —*Aristotle*

Informal recognition is more flexible and spontaneous. An example of this might be a note of thanks for a job well done or acknowledgment at a staff meeting. "Thank you" is a very powerful expression. Everyone knows how to say it, but do they do it? Although texts and e-mails are much faster, realize that the *e* in *e-mail* often stands for *easy*.

> People often say that motivation doesn't last. Well, neither does bathing—that's why we recommend it daily.
>
> —*Zig Ziglar*

People like to receive handwritten notes—it is seen as a much more permanent form of communication. Make it a habit to give spontaneous praise, but also schedule time to write thank-you notes. Every few days, reflect on the good things you have observed and let those people know you appreciate their efforts. Make sure that everyone gets a note at some time during the year or semester. If you can't think of something nice to say to someone . . . why not?

How do you make sure you are giving enough praise? Give a high five. Look around each day, and find five people that deserve a compliment. Then, give them one. Count the five compliments on your hand and make sure you have given them all out before moving on to another activity.

Giving recognition requires a certain degree of mindfulness. It needs to be all of the following:

Timely—Don't delay praise. The recognition needs to be given near the time of the performance. Waiting to give the recognition at the end of the school year may cause it to lose its impact, but if it's delivered in a timely fashion, the recognition could continually motivate the individual and other staff members throughout the year.

Sincere—The recognition needs to be genuine: give it only when it is deserved. Giving an across-the-board recognition lacks sincerity.

Specific—Recognition is a process, not a product. People have told me that their school's recognition program consists of giving all staff members a "You Are Appreciated" mug, card, or other product during staff appreciation week. How special do you feel when everyone is given the exact same thing on a specified day on the calendar? What is the individual being appreciated for? What behavior are you praising? Specify what the staff member worked on and what he or she accomplished.

There are some wonderful recognition products available, and I highly recommend that every supervisor create a Pause for Applause drawer. Keep a supply of recognition items on hand to spontaneously give to staff members for achievements. The items might include Thank You, You Are Appreciated, and Teamwork certificates, pins, notepads, coffee cups, tote bags, pens, water bottles, mouse pads, and so on, which can be ordered from companies such as Positive Promotions (www.positivepromotions.com) and others. You can keep a stock of candy bars, buttons, and stickers as well. Then, when the moment is right, you can choose something that's perfect for the occasion.

Positive—Don't add a *but* when giving the praise. Deliver only a compliment.

You will likely find that staff members are more motivated by informal incentives than by formal ones. They want spontaneous recognition based on their performance rather than an award for something such as years of service.

Not all administrators give recognition. Some people may need to practice giving praise. They may have not been raised with it, may not have had role models, or may simply lack the skills. Those who are most comfortable giving praise typically had parents who used recognition techniques.

Others feel that giving recognition is not part of their job description. Whose responsibility is it then? Actually, it is everyone's.

Peer recognition is very powerful, but staff members also need top-down recognition. If the superintendent and Board of Education value recognition, it becomes a priority. Make it a district goal, and have each school or department develop a yearly recognition plan. Each week, have the administrators give examples of how they recognized their staff. Make this an accountable activity.

Some people might claim they don't have time to give praise and recognition, but that's just an excuse. You make time for the things you value. Most of the types of praise that employees rate as the most motivating—such as personal notes, verbal words of praise, and so on—don't take much time. If you sometimes feel awkward expressing appreciation, rest assured that there is hope. This book abounds with ideas that can help you and your colleagues develop the ability to comfortably give recognition and appreciation. One small step you can take right away is to say that staff members work *with* you, not *for* you. This is especially valuable when you are introducing people from the staff to others. Just a change in those words will have a big impact. Another idea is to add a dash of theater to the praise—make it a fun, glorious event (if you know the recipient will appreciate the display). And if you truly are not a fun person, then allow others to lead in this endeavor: it needs to happen with you or in spite of you.

> You can hire people to work for you, but you must win their hearts to have them work with you.
>
> —Anthony Jay

> Recognition is so easy to do and so inexpensive to distribute that there is no excuse for not doing it.
>
> —Rosabeth Moss Kanter

Here is my best advice for developing a recognition plan:

1. **Staff members should be part of the development and implementation of the plan.** Form a group that has representatives from all employee groups (e.g., teachers, administrative assistants, custodians, those that work in transportation). The group is then responsible for the successes and the things that were not big hits.

2. **The program should be visible to others—both internally to co-workers and students and externally to parents and the community.**

3. **Change the program often so that it stays fresh with new ideas and activities.** Doing the same things becomes routine and expected—an entitlement rather than a reward. Keep the creativity alive and fun.

4. **Recognition and rewards need to be given in a variety of forms, depending on the individual.** Each person is unique and, because of that, the way people want to be treated varies.

> The best recognition programs inspire people to new levels of performance, helping the ordinary people attain extraordinary results in the workplace.
>
> —Bob Nelson

One size does not fit most. It is important to know colleagues and how they like to be recognized. Some people are auditory, some are visual, and others are kinesthetically oriented. And some are a combination of the three.

Auditory—People in this category like to *hear* their recognition. They are the ones who like compliments and want their praise to be public, so give public praise to those who like to be recognized that way. One of the goals is to encourage the individual staff member while also encouraging others to make greater efforts. Praising in public is a good way to raise general morale.

Make it a habit to give compliments every day. You will find that you think wonderful thoughts but frequently don't tell the person. As Ken Blanchard said, "Good thoughts not delivered mean squat." Make a difference in someone's day and see the effect it has on you . . . and others.

As you begin to be more aware of giving compliments, you will see an increase in the number of compliments you receive. It will take practice for you to accept these compliments. We are conditioned from an early age not to brag. If we promoted ourselves by saying things such as "I can run really fast" or "I look great in this new outfit," inevitably someone would say, "Stop bragging." So we tend to feel embarrassed when someone gives us a compliment. We do not have enough practice in receiving this type of praise to feel comfortable.

Most of us will deny or deflect compliments. For instance, if someone tells you, "Your outfit looks great on you," how would you respond? Ideally, you would respond by saying something like, "Thank you. I really feel good when I wear this!" But it's more likely that you would deny the compliment by saying something such as "I do not" or "This old thing? I got it on sale" or "It looked a lot a better on me 10 pounds ago." You may find yourself deflecting the compliment by returning a compliment, "So does yours . . . really . . . you look great." We need to practice receiving and learn how to accept compliments. Enjoy your applause.

Visual—You will recognize these people. They are the ones who look up their names when the new phone book is delivered. They want to find their name in print and see if it is spelled correctly. They like to *see* their recognition. These people want their appreciation to be in the form of a physical item such as a certificate, plaque, letter, card, award, memo, or gift. With these people, there is a lot of give and take. If you *give* recognition such as a certificate, then they want you to *take* a picture. They want this recognition event to be captured and displayed in the staff lounge, district newsletter, local newspaper, or on the bulletin board. They want others to see their recognition and to comment on it.

Kinesthetic—These people are more touch oriented. They need to have a sensory experience through physical connection and motion. They like to have appreciation conveyed through a pat on the back or a handshake. These people are often the ones who like to hug, but hugging can be misconstrued as sexual harassment, so be careful if you express appreciation in this way.

So let's take a little test. Look at the cartoon. What is she? Auditory? Visual? Kinesthetic?

© Aaron Bacall

I am sure the principal thought he was doing something very nice for the administrative assistant. He was likely thinking that when she turned on her computer in the morning, she would be greeted with a "Thank you." In reality, it was not as well received as he imagined. What did she want him to do? She wanted to *hear* his words of thanks—she wanted him to come out of his office and personally deliver the message.

How do you know how each person wants to be recognized? Ask them! At the start of the school year, ask staff members to complete a form about themselves, such as the one shown here.

> With so many ways to reward people, you may ask, "How do I decide how to reward each person?" The answer is simple: Ask them.
>
> —*Michael LeBoeuf*

Creating a Fun, Rewarding School Climate 9

WHEN WE PAUSE FOR APPLAUSE!

Tell us about you . . .

☆ How do you like to be recognized? I am . . .

- ☐ Auditory—I like to *hear* the praise (e.g., compliment)
  - ☐ Privately
  - ☐ Publically
  - ☐ Both

- ☐ Visual—I like to *see* my recognition
  - ☐ Privately—personal notes, sticky notes, and so on
  - ☐ Publically—published praise in newsletters, bulletin boards, lounge, Web page, and so on
  - ☐ Both

- ☐ Kinesthetic—I like to *feel* my recognition
  - ☐ Handshake
  - ☐ Pat on the back
  - ☐ Hug

I feel more motivated when I receive recognition from . . .
- ☐ My peers
- ☐ My principal or supervisor
- ☐ Both

What is your favorite . . .

Candy? _____

Snack food? _____

Salty food? _____

Soft drink? _____

What kind of treat don't you like? _____

What is your favorite type of music? _____

☆ What are your hobbies or interests? _____

Keep the forms on file as a reference in an easily accessible location. Then, when you or other colleagues want to show recognition to a staff member, refer to the information to find the perfect way to do it. As new staff members are hired, include this form as part of the orientation process.

FUN

Another way to motivate staff members is to create a work environment that is fun. Dale Carnegie said, "People rarely succeed unless they have fun in what they are doing." A common misconception is that if you are having fun, then you aren't working. I once heard a speaker say, "If you want to have fun at work, then work at Disney World—don't look for it in a school." Oh my! Many people suffer from the disease of being too serious.

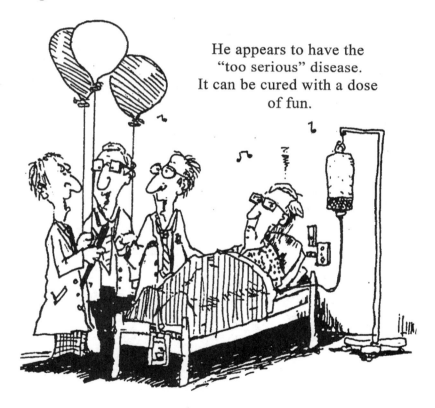

He appears to have the "too serious" disease. It can be cured with a dose of fun.

It is possible to be professional, achieve goals, and enjoy your way to success. Could it be that when you incorporate fun into the workplace, the result will be an increase in teamwork, a decrease in absenteeism ("Monday migraines"), reduced stress, and an improved sense of balance between personal and professional lives? As many organizations are reporting, the answer is YES! Would a person feel revitalized in an organization where there was excitement, support, and celebrations? Would there be an increase in staff morale and productivity? Again—YES! Laughter and play help colleagues to connect because they speak a common language of joy.

> After you've laughed together, you're much more tolerant of each other.
>
> —Matt Weinstein

We spend more time at work than anywhere else, so we should enjoy our work life. In order to have a fun working environment, you have to have fun people working there. I travel a great deal, and it seems that to get from San Diego to anywhere, I have to go through O'Hare Airport in Chicago. The process of going through security can often be tedious. On one trip, I gave my identification to a TSA employee, and when she returned it, she smiled and said, "Have a marvelous Monday." As the author of *Looking Forward to Monday Morning*, I was taken aback. I asked her what she would have said if it had been a Tuesday. She said she has a response for each day of the week. She proceeded to tell me all of them.

- *Marvelous* Monday
- *Terrific* Tuesday
- *Wonderful* Wednesday
- *Tremendous* Thursday
- *Fabulous* Friday
- *Sensational* Saturday
- *Super* Sunday

She put a smile on everyone's face by sharing her positive attitude—and she seemed to genuinely enjoy her job.

It is important to hire fun people. When you post an open job, list *sense of humor* as one of the qualities you are seeking. Include *fun* in the job interview. For example, give the interviewees some Silly Putty and see how they react. Ask them to tell you a clean joke, ask them to describe their ideal work environment, or ask them to share how they once added humor to a stressful situation. Have the candidate work for a day with staff to see how they fit in.

If you want to attract fun people to work at your school, then you need to let the community know that your workplace is fun. Report "April Fools," "Human Sundae," and other fun events in your local and district newsletter. Word will spread. When you are creating or revising your mission statement, include all of the essentials and end it with a statement such as "and enjoy the journey."

The best way to infuse fun into an organization is by example. But what if you have a boss who isn't fun? What if you are convinced that he or she would never plan and implement a fun activity? Two teachers spoke with me after one of my presentations. They shared that they had a new principal and the climate had changed from fun to glum. One said, "We are just going to have to have fun in spite of him. We will be the Ambassadors of Fun for the school." As they left, I heard one say, "Today was the first time I have laughed in two weeks." If you are facing a similar situation, appoint yourself as one of the following:

CHO (Chief Happiness Officer)

Manager of Mirth

Ambassador of Play

Director of Positive Attitudes

Funmeister

Minister of Fun

Pep King or Queen

Director of WOW

Or gather other fun people and brand yourselves as one of the following:

Joy Gang

Mirth Committee

Fun Committee

Cheer Committee

Happiness Group

Carol Kahler, principal of Gilbert Linkous Elementary School in Blacksburg, Virginia, has an in-house committee called "The Happy, Peppy Club." This name came from the *I Love Lucy* show, where Lucy was the *Vitameatavegemin Girl* trying to sell a vitamin concoction to boost energy. "So why don't you join the thousands of happy peppy people and get a great big bottle of Vitameatavegemin tomorrow," she said in her sales pitch. Kahler says her group "helps with door prizes, seating assignments at meetings to have staff members sit with new colleagues, icebreakers, etc."

If you aren't a fun person, you can contribute to a fun work environment just by letting others implement fun activities. Schedule the first Fun Committee meeting, elect a chairperson, and let the group put together the yearly plan.

How do staff members like to have fun? Ask them. Make a *Fun Suggestion Box*, where they can contribute ideas for activities. On the suggestion form, ask if the person is willing to organize the activity.

Get together outside of work too. Put the events on the calendar to ensure that they actually happen.

Go to a comedy club

Organize a beach party

Go bowling

Play miniature golf

Go skiing

Go to a movie

Go to the gym

 # FUNDRAISERS

Often, people ask, "How can we fund the recognition activities?" Many valued recognition activities, such as giving personal words of praise and writing thank-you notes, don't cost anything, but others do. I am a firm believer that it should not cost workers money to do their jobs. I am always amazed at how much of their own money educators spend on school-related activities. It took me a while, but I learned that if you want something, you should ask for it. Develop your recognition plan and estimate how much each event will cost. You probably won't have much district money to work with, so ask local businesses, community organizations, and parent groups to sponsor the events. Sometimes you may feel like you are begging when you ask for contributions. I spoke at a conference where they had a large number of door prizes that had been donated by area businesses. The chairperson of the committee said that she called the manager of a local chocolate production site. She asked if he would donate chocolate as a prize. After school, she drove to the factory, located the manager, and he gave her chocolate—one bar! Be sure that when you ask for donations, you give the company an idea of what you would like. Here are some suggestions:

- Box of chocolate
- Supply of postage stamps
- Dry cleaning coupon
- Savings bond
- Software to use at home
- House cleaning service for a day
- Car wash coupons
- Free income tax preparation
- Free tutoring for your child
- Dozen cookies
- Massage coupon
- Pedicure coupon
- Haircut coupon
- Manicure coupon
- Tickets to a sporting event
- Free session with a financial planner
- Weekend hotel certificate
- Free pair of shoes
- Movie passes
- Grooming for your pet
- Automobile detailing
- Free book at a local bookstore
- Dental whitening from a dentist
- Professional development activity
- Garden supplies
- Beach towels and suntan lotion
- Eyeglass frames
- Holiday dinner in a basket

Sponsorships can take the form of a monetary donation, or the sponsor can plan and implement the event. Be sure to give the organizations plenty of recognition for the activities they contribute to—and remember to invite them to the events they're sponsoring. I spoke at a wonderful opening day staff breakfast event for a district in which over a thousand staff members attended. The event was totally funded by a local financial institution.

It is sometimes harder to get donations for fun activities, so you can conduct simple FUNdraisers among your staff or in your community. These are some of the easy things you can do to fund your fun or recognition events.

Campus FUNdraisers

Personal Business Day Raffle

Most professional contracts allow staff members to have a designated number of personal business days—days in which they can take care of things that need to be handled during the day. In an informal survey of my audiences, I ask the participants what is most important to them. The response is the same across the entire country—TIME!

On the first day of school, sell raffle tickets for staff members to win a personal business day. Sell tickets throughout the day, particularly during lunch. If you have more than one preservice day, then sell tickets each day. At the end of the day(s), select the winning ticket at an event where all staff members are present.

You could also do another raffle during the second semester, when a day off in the middle of winter might just raise a lot of money.

Help Has Arrived Lottery

Sell lottery tickets to staff members. Draw tickets to select the winner(s). The winner gets the superintendent or principal as an assistant for a half of a day.

Dress Down Days

Designate Dress Down Days on which staff members may wear jeans and casual dress rather than their professional attire. Staff members donate three dollars (or another designated amount) for a button or ribbon to wear explaining why they're dressed differently that day.

Dessert Taste-Off

Ask staff members to prepare their favorite desserts during October for National Dessert Month. Make a display of all the entries and provide napkins, plates, and forks. Place a container behind each entry and assign it a number (and list the type of dessert displayed so the containers aren't moved). Don't include information about the dessert's creator. Throughout the day or during lunch times, staff members can taste the desserts and vote for their favorite(s) by putting coins in the cans of the desserts they enjoyed the most.

If you have a large staff, plan two dessert days. Have the staff members with last names beginning with the letters A through K prepare desserts for the first event and those with last names beginning with the letters L through Z prepare desserts for the second dessert day. Staff members may prepare desserts for both days if they wish. *(Darlene Roll, Ohio High-Point Career Center, Bellefontaine, OH)* The winner gets a certificate or other dessert-related item, and the money in the cans goes into the recognition and fun fund.

Chili Cook-Off

Invite staff members to prepare their favorite versions of chili. Have staff members purchase tasting tickets and vote for their favorite recipes. Make the portion sizes large enough that they receive a full lunch. Do not identify the people who made each chili. The winners get a basket of hot sauces or another food-related prize.

You could have the voting occur as described in the Dessert Taste-Off and have several days of competition.

Bring One-Buy One Sale

Have a sale where staff members both provide an item to be sold and purchase an item from the sale. In theory, at the end of the day nothing will be left. If there are remaining items, donate them to charity.

If you want to expand this FUNdraising activity, make it a community-wide event. It can be hosted at the school or at a community center. You may charge an admission fee, which will add to the day's revenue.

Potluck Breakfasts and Lunches

Create themes for breakfast and lunch events throughout the year. Have volunteer staff members bring in food that reflects the themes. You can also ask local restaurants to donate food items for the events. Sell tickets to staff members for four dollars for breakfast and five dollars for lunch. Hold the breakfast events before school; for lunches, have the administrators cover lunch duty so teachers can eat together away from students and the cafeteria. "We always raised several hundred dollars from these events as well as teachers loved the time together. We did these FUNdraisers several times a year, and they were a huge hit!" *(Dana Carlton, Cobb County Schools, Marietta, GA)*

PANCAKE BREAKFAST!

Basket Silent Auction

Ask staff members to make theme baskets. An example of a theme might be Movie Night. The basket could contain items such as a DVD, a video store gift certificate or card, popcorn, candy, soda, or a fleece blanket. Staff members can ask community businesses to donate some items to the basket. Other themes might include the following:

- Coffee Lovers—flavored coffees, coffee mug, biscotti, flavored stir sticks, and chocolate spoons
- Chocolate Lovers—lots of chocolate
- Chocolates of the World—an assortment of chocolates from countries around the world, such as Toblerone (Switzerland), Lindt (Europe), and Milka (Germany)
- Spa at Home—bath salts, spa music, lotion, scented candles, and a pedicure coupon
- Are We There Yet?—travel items such as games, snacks, maps, a flashlight, and aspirin
- Are We Having Fun Yet?—yo-yos, crossword puzzles, movie gift cards, deck of cards, and a board game
- Classroom in a Box—a box of school supplies, including markers, stickers, and tape
- Olé! Mexican Vacation—salsa, chips, margarita glasses, and suntan lotion
- Luck in a Basket—chocolate coins, lottery tickets, and so on
- Snack Attack—chips, granola bars, juice boxes, microwave popcorn, and fruit
- Sports Lover—*Sports Illustrated,* sporting event tickets, whistle, baseball cap, hand warmers, hot dog magnet, and bleacher seat cushions
- Holiday Basket—a basket appropriate for the nearest holiday, such as Valentine's Day or Halloween
- Breakfast in Bed—coffee cup with a coffee and tea bag inside, bagels, fruit, a magazine, a vase with a rose, and a linen napkin
- Book Lover—paperback books, bookmarks, magnifying glasses, snacks, magazines, a book light, a bookstore gift card, and highlighters
- Car Wash—sponges, bucket, shammy cloth, car wash detergent, and gift certificates for a car wash

- Summertime—sunscreen, sunglasses, magazines, beach towel, beach ball, sand bucket and shovel, and drink holders

Place the baskets on display, and put out silent auction sheets so that staff members can bid on the baskets. The highest bidder at the end of the designated period gets to keep the basket. Note: Alcoholic beverages should not be included in the baskets. *(Dana Carlton, Cobb County Schools, Marietta, GA)*

You could also sell raffle tickets to staff members (and parents). Put containers by each of the baskets. Have staff members deposit tickets into the containers that are nearest to the baskets they want. Hold the drawings at the end of the day or week. Select a ticket from each container to determine the winner of each basket.

Festival of Wreaths

You could have another raffle with holiday wreaths. Businesses could make and donate the wreaths, individual classrooms could make them, or staff members could create them. One particularly clever one that I saw in a nursing home was made by elementary students. The theme was Peace on Earth, and it was decorated with puzzle pieces. Raffle off the wreaths to be enjoyed in community members' homes.

Fine for FUN!

Late for a staff meeting? Late getting your lesson plans in? Late with your grades? Determine a *lateness fine*. Each time someone is late, assess the fine. The money collected goes into the FUNdraising fund.

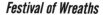

Keep it Positive

Designate Monday as *Positive Day.* Everything said that day has to be just that—positive. There is no complaining about the weather over the weekend, the sports team that lost, housecleaning and laundry, or anything else. Anyone who is caught saying anything negative is fined a designated amount.

Spare Change

Decorate receptacles, such as birdhouses, and place them near the vending machine and in cafeteria lines. Label them with *Spare Change Fund*. Have staff members donate their spare change to the recognition fund. Each month, post the total for the month's contributions.

Variation

During one week, put out a jar where staff members congregate. Ask everyone to contribute their change as donations. Collect a different denomination each day.

Monday—pennies

Tuesday—nickels

Wednesday—dimes

Thursday—quarters

Friday—paper bills

Staff Bingo

Coordinate with a local restaurant to have a staff bingo night. Often, the restaurant will provide complimentary appetizers. Have staff members purchase bingo cards for each game. The winners receive a portion of the proceeds and have the choice of keeping their winnings or donating them to the FUNdraising campaign. Of course, most donate! *(Dana Carlton, Cobb County Schools, Marietta, GA)* You could coordinate this with National Bingo month, which is December.

Holiday Shopping

Invite independent consultants or representatives of products and companies, such as Pampered Chef, Mary Kay, purse and shoe consultants, Tupperware, and so on, to show their products at an afterschool event. The sales representatives donate all or part of their commission to the FUNdraising event. This is especially successful when held at the start of the holiday shopping season and again prior to Mother's Day. *(Dana Carlton, Cobb County Schools, Marietta, GA)*

Fuzzy Flip-Flops

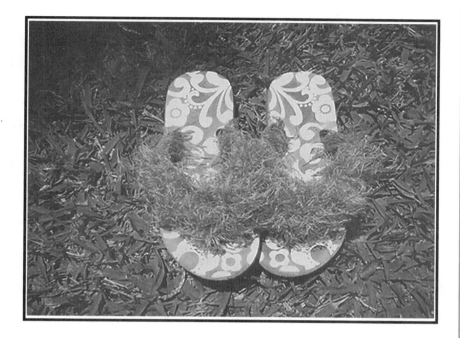

Ask volunteers to crochet flip-flops with fuzzy yarn, and then sell them. You could start a new style trend! Save them for the spring and use them with the staff appreciation event found in Chapter 5 (Sensational Spring) titled "We Have Flipped Over Our Staff."

Age Game

Hold a contest in which staff members guess the combined ages of the administrators. For each guess, staff members donate a designated amount of money toward the fun events. The winner is given a prize. If you have more than one person with the correct answer, put all the correct answers in a hat and draw one winner.

How Many?

You can incorporate this FUNdraiser a number of times during the year, especially during the holidays. Fill a jar with treats, such as candy kisses for Valentine's Day, candy corn at Halloween, or peppermint candy at Christmas. Have staff members donate an amount of money each time they submit a guess as to how many pieces of candy are in the jar. The person who guesses a number closest to the actual number of candies in the jar gets to keep the jar—and all of the candy!

Splitting the Take

Begin staff meetings with a 50/50 drawing, where people can buy a raffle ticket for one dollar. A duplicate-numbered ticket is put into a container. A ticket is drawn from the container, and the matching-ticket holder receives half of the money collected. The other half goes to the recognition and fun fund.

Staff Meeting Raffle

Raffle off products at staff meetings. Products may be samples donated by a sales representative, a gift from a business partner, or a certificate for a homemade delight prepared by the principal!

Community FUNdraisers

Rent a Graffiti Wall

Many people love to write and draw graffiti. Often, the motivator is not the destruction of property, but rather self-expression. Designate a wall (or walls) on the campus or in the community on which it is OK to express positive emotions. Rent the space for a designated length of time to people or companies to express their love, cheer on their team, make a marriage proposal, give congratulations, promote a product, or anything else that is positive.

Parents Night Out

Plan one evening in which the staff provides child care at the school so the parents can have a night out. During the designated hours, serve dinner, show a movie, and have simple crafts for the children to work on. Charge the parents a fee for the evening. Be sure to have the parents provide their contact information. Let them know that if they are late in picking up their children, they will be charged extra. This event will be especially appreciated prior to the winter holidays.

Chair-ity Auction

You have probably seen the fabulous cows in Chicago that were uniquely decorated, displayed throughout the city, and ultimately auctioned off for charity. Other cities capitalized on this theme and decorated pigs and other items that were unique to their communities. In the same vein, have a *chair*-ity auction. Enlist businesses and community members to buy a chair and decorate it. If your community has a real estate showcase where members of the public view model homes that are decorated by local interior design firms, include the

chairs in the staging of the homes. After the home tour, auction the chairs. The chairs can also be displayed in the windows of retail establishments, in the schools, and so on.

IN CLOSING

Creating a fun, rewarding school climate is everyone's responsibility—we all need to give to others and have fun together. We cannot help but thrive when we are surrounded by motivated, enthusiastic, positive colleagues. Use the ideas in this book to keep you and your coworkers enthusiastic and growing. *Drive your colleagues HAPPY!*

CHAPTER 2

Start of the School Year

BEFORE SCHOOL STARTS—
GET READY!

The planning for the start of the upcoming school year begins
as soon as you catch your breath from closing out the previous
school year. How you begin the year sets the tone for the upcoming
months. You are going to want to have fun, motivating, invigorating
activities that help the staff members make the transition from summer
to the school year. It is a bit of a shock to the system at first.

Summer E-mails

Often, there is silence between the administrators and the staff
members over the summer. Send e-mails to just say "hi," to
let them know of any changes that have taken place at the district or
building level, to pass along information about their peers, and so on.
Be sure to include the bios of new staff members so that returning
staff members are prepared to give them a warm, heartfelt
welcome.

Summer Update Chain Letter

Staff members frequently lose touch with each other over
the summer and often wonder what their peers are up to.
Make a list of all the staff members and their e-mail addresses.
Compose a survey e-mail that asks about their summer activities.
Have the staff member who receives the e-mail copy the questions and
answer them. Then, ask that the survey be sent to the next person in
the staff directory. Have the last person on the list forward it to the first
person on the list (see questionnaire on page 27). Add your own
questions to the list.

Travel Postcards

When you are out of town attending a conference, purchase
postcards from the host city. Send them to colleagues to let
them know that you are at a professional development event
and hope they have a summer full of renewal and rejuvenation
that brings energy to the start of the year. (*Kristina Brunson, RQ Sims
Intermediate School District, Mexia, TX*)

SUMMER QUESTIONNAIRE

Name _____

1. What was the most fun thing you did this summer?

2. Did you do any traveling? If so, where did you go?

3. Are you working somewhere? If so, where?

4. Did you read a good book that you would recommend to others?

5. Did you go to a movie or rent a "must see" DVD?

6. Did you take classes or attend a conference? (If so, give details.)

7. Did you play any sports?

8. Did you make any changes? New hair style, weight loss?

9. Are you hosting visitors?

10. Do you have a funny story to share?

11. What's the most disastrous thing that happened this summer?

12. What do you love most about being off for the summer?

13. What do you miss most about not being at work?

14. Do you have any kudos about a colleague's activities over the summer?

15. Do you know of any colleague who needs a word of encouragement?

Return Directions: Copy this entire e-mail and paste it into a new e-mail that you will send. (Do not delete the entries by other staff members.) Change all of the answers so they apply to you. Then send the e-mail to the staff member whose name is below yours on the list. If you are the last person on the list, send it to the first person so the results make a complete circle.

GET SET!

Caption It!

Collect cartoons or pictures that relate to the summer or start of school. Remove any captions that go with the pictures.

When you send your back-to-school letter to staff members, enclose the pictures and ask that staff members write their own captions. Ask that they be brought in on the first day to be shared with others.

Post each picture on a large piece of shelf paper with plenty of extra room for writing. Have a supply of markers handy so staff members can write in their captions. You can either have staff members identify their captions or have them be anonymous. You could make a contest out of it and have staff members vote for the best captions.

On Your Mark . . . Get Set . . . Shop!

In recognition of achievements from the previous year, invite staff members to meet for an outing. Arrange for a bus to take them to an area shopping mall. Assemble all of the staff members on the bus and give each person 100 dollars in cash. Tell them that they will have one hour to spend the money, *but* the money can be spent only on items for themselves *and* they cannot exceed 100 dollars. When everyone arrives at the mall, call out "On your mark . . . Get set . . . Shop!"

After the hour, assemble the staff on the bus and ask them to share what they purchased and how close they were able to get to the 100 dollar mark. The person(s) who came closest to 100 dollars without going over is the winner and receives a small prize. This is an expensive event, but one that will be remembered!

Planning Retreat

Many retreat centers have reasonable or complimentary rates for educational groups. Going to an off-site location reduces distractions and focuses staff members' attention on the year ahead. Plan working events that allow staff members to bond, offer a mix of socialization and team-building activities, and make time for the staff to reach agreement on the goals for the new school year and plan how to work together to achieve them. Invite a motivational speaker to get the staff enthused and to boost their spirits.

While at the retreat, also plan leisure activities. Have staff members volunteer to teach others how to do something not related to school, such as yoga, line dancing, or juggling. Have them share how they spend their time outside of school. Plan group walks and enjoy the environment.

You may get community sponsors to donate products that serve as door prizes (or are included in goodie bags). The bags could be filled with items such as teaching supplies, professional reading materials, or a school calendar—things recipients could use in their jobs.

You could also prepare a "Me Kit" for each staff member. The kit would contain things that will bring comfort to staff members or will

help them if they are in need. Items to include might be a sewing kit, safety pins, adhesive bandages, cough drops, breath mints, mouthwash, greeting cards, or treats (chocolate, salty snack, candy bar, etc.). Then, when people are having "one of those days," these little helpers are ready.

This type of event also leads to another result: new staff members begin to feel part of the group and veterans feel recommitted to their jobs and colleagues.

Road Rally

Divide the staff into groups of four or five members so they can ride together in a car. Make a list of people they need to find and have their picture taken with. Set a time limit. Assign points for each picture. For example:

- Picture with the mayor = 25 points
- Picture with a former principal = 30 points
- Picture with a security guard = 20 points

Have the teams video record their road rally and bring the recording back to the school. The videos could be shown and judged, and prizes could be awarded for the most points achieved, the most creative video, and so on. Or you could save the videos and show them on the last staff day of the school year.

Back to School Day

Many staff members return to school before their contracted start date to set up their rooms and get everything ready for the students' arrival. Send an e-mail to the staff announcing a voluntary *Back to School Day*. Let them know that if they want to work in their room or office, food and drinks will be available throughout the day. Arrange to have some high school students and community volunteers available to assist them on that day.

Give each staff member who participates in the day a coupon for a "Welcome Back Bag." Staff members may then bring the coupon to the office, catch up on the summer's activities, and receive a bag of goodies. The bag of goodies could be snack foods, school supplies, a CD of music to work to, coupons to restaurants, an early release pass to use during the year, or a casual dress certificate for a day of their choice—a little reward for the unpaid time they are giving for students.

Helping Hand Day

Starting as a new staff member in a school or district can be daunting. There is a huge learning curve, which means it takes longer for a new employee to get settled into a new year than it does veteran staff members. Invite the new staff members to come in early for an orientation to alleviate their anxiety. Take them on a tour of the school, introduce them to staff members who are working, show them how to order supplies and get their mail, and let them get the lay of the land.

Set a date toward the end of the summer, and e-mail staff members about participating in a voluntary *Helping Hand Day.* Staff members may volunteer to come in before school starts to help new teachers set up their rooms and get acclimated to the new school.

Custodian Banner

Often, the custodians are unsung heroes. They work all summer to get the schools ready for the start of the school year. They are at work when few people are around and often don't receive the accolades they deserve. Hang a banner at the entrance of the school that remains on display throughout the year. Have the following printed on the banner: *Our school is beautifully maintained by . . . ,* and list the names of the custodial staff members.

OUR SCHOOL IS BEAUTIFULLY MAINTAINED BY SAM DAUGHERTY, JOSE GARCIA, AND SARAH JONES

Children need all school workers. A person is not "just" a janitor, not "just" a custodian. Janitors can see children when (teachers) don't see them, and bus drivers recognize that children who are disruptive on the bus are likely to be disorderly in the classroom. They're partners in education. We need each other to make this work.

—*Reverend Jesse Jackson*

GO! READY OR NOT . . . HERE THEY COME!

As you walk through the school, there is a silence that you will not hear again for many months. The school looks the best it will ever look: the floors are glowing from the newly applied wax and buffing, the windows are shining, and there is not a piece of trash to be found. The furniture is placed with precision, and there is a sense of calm. But schools are more than buildings, furniture, equipment, and books. Schools are relationships and interactions between multiple groups of people. Soon the calm will be broken with a flurry of activity and the quiet will disappear—but then, this is the way schools are meant to be.

Wake-Up Calls

On the first day of school, have wake-up calls made to each of your staff members who have been away from the school all summer. Log onto www.mrwakeup.com. You can record a message that says something positive and uplifting, such as "Good morning, Tina. You have been missed this summer. We will all be looking forward to seeing you today and know we are going to have a fabulous new year!" The staff member will receive the phone call as a nice way to start the day and year.

Sing-Along

It is a shock to come back on the first day of school. Eric Baylin, a teacher at the Packer Collegiate Institute in Brooklyn, New York, understands the reentry process and what an abrupt change it is from the low gear of summer to the high gear of the new school year. Have a staff sing-along and start the year with some fun!

Seems Like We Were Never Gone
(Sung to the tune of "Get Back" by the Beatles)

Summer came around; we thought it
    would be longer,
But we knew it couldn't last.
Would have liked another week or
    two or longer.
Now we gotta get to class.

We're back, we're back,
We're back here where we all belong.
We're back, we're back,
It seems like we were never gone.

Some had big adventures trips to
    Greece and Turkey,
Others slept beside the pool.
Minds were far away from school and
    all the work. We
Needed summer to re-fuel.

We're back, we're back,
We're back here where we all belong.
We're back, we're back,
It seems like we were never gone.

With the start of school, we're feeling
    apprehensive,
What will come our way this year?
If we don't take care, we'll end up
    getting tense if
We forget our sense of cheer.

We're back, we're back,
We're back here where we all belong.
We're back, we're back,
It seems like we were never gone.

How to keep the ease of summertime
    inside us,
That's the challenge we all face.
Better not to dwell on how our last
    year fried us,
Find some quiet time and space.

We're back, we're back,
We're back here
    we all belong.
We're back, we're back,
It seems like we were never gone.

Fill the year with pedagogical
    adventures,
Find the moments ripe to seize.
Keep the flame of learning burning,
    never quench your
Thirst for possibilities.

We're back, we're back,
We're back here where we all belong.
We're back, we're back,
It seems like we were never gone.

Summer Whines

The end of summer is not entirely a bad thing. It also brings to an end the whining that staff members heard from their children over the summer. Examples of "summer whines" might include "There's nothing to do. I'm bored. We're hot. It's summer—we don't have to go to bed early." Post a large sheet of chart paper in the staff lounge and let them write their summer whines on it. You may want to share them at your first staff meeting.

New Year Party

Send staff members invitations to a New Year Party to be held the first day of school. Greet the staff by wearing formal attire, such as a tuxedo or gown, and give them party hats, small paper horns, party streamers, and plastic champagne glasses filled with candy or nuts as party favors. Decorate the room where they will be meeting with New Year banners and have great dance music playing in the background. Encourage the staff members to dance and throw their party streamers. Print the agenda for the day on New Year themed paper. When staff members hear something they like or agree with what is being said, have them blow their horns to show agreement. When the clock strikes 12:00 (noon) have a "Noon Year" celebration and sing "Auld Lang Syne," blow the horns, and serve nonalcoholic fruit juice to toast and celebrate the New Year. *(Patti Kenworthy, Stevensville, MI)*

You may want to have staff members grab a spoon and toast the New Year with a cool, sparkly dessert that wiggles. Make bubbly Jell-O according to the directions on the box of fruit-flavored Jell-O. Use club soda, seltzer, or ginger ale. Chill the gelatin in champagne flutes, which can be made the day before the start of school. You can decorate the stems of the flutes with star garlands, which are available at party stores, to add to the festiveness.

You're Invited!!

To Celebrate the New Year

When: August 25

Where: High School Cafeteria

Time: 8:30 a.m. to 12:00 p.m.

Dress: Casual and Comfortable

This is a BYOP event (Bring Your Own Pen or Pencil)

See you then!!

Happy New School!

Are you opening a new school? This is the perfect time to have a Happy New School theme for both staff members and students. Decorate the entire school in festive New Year décor, and include a lot of getting-to-know-you activities. *(Carol Leveille, Mary B. Neal Elementary School, Waldorf, MD)*

Amazing Race

This activity allows staff members to bond and to get to know the community. Split them into teams of five to seven members, ensuring that unfamiliar people are grouped together or that there is a cross-section of grade levels or curricular areas represented in each group. Give each team color-coded hats, bandanas, backpacks, and sunglasses. (You can find these items at Oriental Trading Company, www.orientaltrading.com.) Have each team select a team name and designate someone as a driver. Give each team a list of 12 stations they have to visit in your community. When the teams visit these locations, they are to bring back proof that they were actually there.

Staff members at Richard Gordon Elementary School carved small paddles at the local Indian reservations, spun pizza dough, hit a bucket of balls at the new golf course, visited the food bank, and so on. The day ended with all groups meeting at one location for a beverage, where they shared the stories of their adventures. "It took a *lot* of planning on my part, but it was worth every minute." *(Claudia Alves, Richard Gordon Elementary School, Kingston, WA)*

A Week of Fun

Involve the students in daily activities that are designed to welcome the staff back. For example, prepare popcorn for the staff members to enjoy during their breaks. The next day, make ice cream floats as a special treat. You could also have Wii sports competitions for added fun. *(Karen Koehn, Northwest Technology Center, Alva, OK)*

A Star Event

The night before staff members arrive for the first day of school, leave a note in each staff member's room with a personalized compliment on paper titled "Wishing You a Stellar Year."

While wearing top hats and white gloves, roll out the red carpet for the "Star-Studded Staff." While star-themed music plays in the background, have the administrators stand in front of the school with clappers and whistles and greet each staff member with a star-shaped balloon. Have the administrators open the doors to the school, which is decorated in a Hollywood theme. Later in the day, the staff members are treated to a lunch of super-star salads.

At the opening staff meeting, give all staff members a paper that says, "I Am a Star!" and then tape that to their backs. While more star-themed music plays in the background, have staff members write positive comments on the papers taped to their colleagues' backs. Afterward, have each person remove his or her paper and read the positive statements. It makes for a nice keepsake.

Use the theme throughout the year, including a "Super Stars" section in the weekly newsletter that acknowledges staff member achievements. *(Amy Cashwell, Christopher Farms Elementary School, Virginia Beach, VA)*

A Sweet Welcome

Welcome back staff and students by making a creative bulletin board. Use the wrappers from packages of candy and gum as part of the text in the message.

Sleepy Hollow Elementary School prepared this bulletin board for the start of the school year. (The text is shown on page 37.)

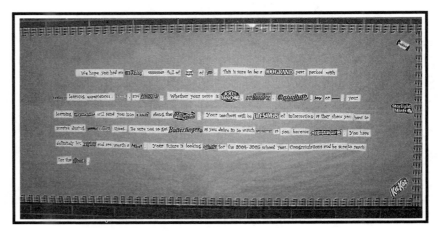

Photo provided by Anastasia Epstein, Sleepy Hollow Elementary School, Sleepy Hollow, IL

Welcome Back,

We hope you had an *M-azing* summer full of Good and Plenty of fun. This is sure to be a 100 Grand year packed with Extra learning experiences, Chuckles, and Snickers. Whether your name is Jolly Rancher, Mr. Goodbar, Baby Ruth, or Joy, your learning Spree will send you into Orbit along the Milky Way. Your teachers will be Life Savers of information as they show you how to survive during Crunch times. Be sure not to get Butterfingers as you delve in to watch Starbursts as you become Smarties. You have definitely hit Pay Day and are worth a mint. Your future is looking Brite for the school year. Congratulations and be sure to reach for the Stars.

Photo Scavenger Hunt

Begin the school year with a Photo Scavenger Hunt of your school's community. This event is a fun way for new staff members to get acquainted with their new colleagues and the community, and it is great fun.

Divide the staff members into teams. Tell each team to take a photo (with all members in the picture) for each item on the list. Some items on the list might be each subdivision or apartment complex that attends the school, local business partners, or PTA members. Have the teams write and deliver thank-you notes to local business partners and collect contact information for possible business partners. Create a display of all the pictures. "The parents and students loved seeing their teachers having fun!" *(Lisa Leethem, Bear Creek Elementary School, Houston, TX)*

CHOOSE A THEME!

When the school year is ending, ask the staff to select a theme for the following year. Over the summer and throughout the year, have a team of staff members plan activities that emphasize the theme. Use it in selecting goodies to serve, community donations for door prizes, and skits. A new theme helps staff

members look forward to that year's activities. Examples chosen by schools include:

- Make it Happen!
- Go From Good to Great While Having Fun!
- Do or Do Not . . . There Is No Try!
- The Future of Our Youth Is in Our Hands!
- Be the Best You Can Be!
- We Can See Clearly Now!
- Light the Way to Success!
- Mission Possible!
- Take the Dare!
- Moving Forward!
- Onward and Upward!
- Hand in Hand—Together We Can!
- Bloom Where You Are Planted!
- Racing to Success!
- It's All Good!

Keller Elementary School, in Metairie, Louisiana, incorporates themes into the start of each school year as well as activities throughout the year, including special recognition days, staff members' birthdays, parent group activities, and so on. Past themes have included the following:

- Let Me Take You on a Scenic Cruise—Beach/surfer theme
- Taking the Reins of Education at Keller—Western theme
- Keller Goes to Hollywood—Everyone's a Star theme
- Aloha Keller—Hawaiian theme
- Keller Rocks Around the Clock—1950s theme in which a vodcast invitation was sent with 1950s music and vintage clothes

Principal Sandy Doland shared that "these days and years are positive and fun and meaningful memory makers." *(Sandy Doland, Keller Elementary School, Metairie, LA)*

Git Er Done

Incorporate a Western theme into the school year. Send invitations to the staff inviting them to the first day of school. Design the invitations to represent Wanted Posters. You could send a bandana with the invitation and ask that it be worn to school.

Greet the staff wearing Western attire. You could dress in cowboy or cowgirl attire or be a schoolmarm, sheriff, or rodeo rider. Have Western music playing, such as the theme songs from *Bonanza, Have Gun Will Travel*, and *Rawhide*. Of course, you can have contemporary country music playing, too.

Set up your meeting area with red-and-white checked tablecloths, snakes, cactus, and so on. For lunch, serve ribs, corn bread, chili, and beans—lots of beans. You could have a horseshoe-throwing competition for the break time. It will be a truckload of fun!

Use the *Git Er Done* theme throughout the year as initiatives and due dates arrive.

We're BOB

You have probably seen the "I'm Bob" T-shirts advertised in catalogs or the buildings named BOB—**B**ig **O**ld **B**uilding. Have BOB T-shirts made for staff members—**B**eing **O**ur **B**est. Use the BOB theme throughout the year and allow staff members to wear their T-shirts on Monday mornings if they have had perfect attendance the week before. BOB can also be used as **B**end **O**ver **B**ackward awards for those who go above and beyond in their jobs.

WANTED

BUCKAROO STAFF MEMBERS
Willing to Work Hard
and Make a Difference!

Date~Time~Location
Attire: Western
(cowboy hat, boots, denim skirt, vest, bandana, etc)

B.O.B. WE'RE BEING OUR BEST

BOB WE'RE BEING OUR BEST

The Journey Begins With Us!

One school selected the theme *The Journey Begins With Us*. To create a visual to go along with the theme, each staff member decorated a

star to symbolize that the staff members were all-stars. The stars were used to create a paper quilt that was displayed in the district office. *(Janice Allen, Pasadena Unified School District, Pasadena, CA)* The stars could also be used as a display.

Knock Your Socks Off/Roll With It/King of the Mountain!

Ross Elementary School, in Milford, Delaware, selected the theme *Knock Your Socks Off This Year*. The committee made a banner incorporating the theme. The staff members had to run through the paper banner and break it in order to enter the staff meeting room. When inside, a pair of socks that featured the school logo was placed on each chair for staff members to wear.

    Later in the year, another activity was held that was consistent with the theme *Knock Your Socks Off*. As the time for testing neared, they planned a *Peppermint Soak*. Based on the premise that the aroma of peppermint may help release tension and dissipate fatigue, arrangements were made with a Body Shop consultant who provided peppermint soaks for all the staff members. Staff members soaked and

scrubbed their feet, applied foot gel and lotion, and enjoyed a peppermint mask. "It was an awesome event as a great de-stressor prior to the tests," added Dr. Sylvia Henderson.

    The next year, the theme was *Roll With It*. The red carpet was rolled out, staff members rolled around on scooters, and throughout the year Tootsie Rolls and Life Saver candies were given out. Staff rolled different types of balls and rolled paper into art during a staff meeting as a stress reliever.

    The next theme was *King of the Mountain*. The school ranked

> The time to relax is when you don't have time for it.
>
> —Sidney J. Harris

number one in the state for reading and math scores, so they felt as if they were the *King of the Mountain*. (Of course, there are no mountains in Delaware!) The healthy lifestyle events included hiking and fitness and serving trail mix—things you would do as you climbed a mountain. *(Sylvia Henderson, Ross Elementary School, Milford, DE)*

Taking It Up a Notch!

The theme *Taking It Up a Notch* lends itself to having a cooking theme all year. Have *Taking It Up a Notch* forms printed on No Carbon Required (NCR) paper. Give a supply to all staff members, and when their colleagues do something worthy of a *thank you, way to go,* or *wow,* the message is written on the form. Parents can also submit recognition forms.

Each week, have the administrators don chef's hats and aprons and carry bowls and wooden spoons as noise makers. Have them beat their "drums" to get everyone's attention, whether it's in the staff lounge, hall, or classrooms. The recognitions are read about each staff person for all to hear. The individuals sign the recognition form, and the second copy goes into their appraisal files.

Prizes are awarded. (It also helps to vary the number of times the person has been recognized.)

First recognition: Individuals are given a personalized apron.

Second recognition: Individuals receive a chef's hat pin to put on the apron.

After the second award, staff members receive more chef's hat pins for every even-numbered award they receive.

Each time a person receives recognition, his or her name is put into a jar for a drawing. Throughout the year, names are selected for door prizes so they have the chance to become extra special winners. *(Patricia Paetow, Katy Independent School District, Katy, TX)*

Choose to Fly

Choose to Fly is a theme based on the book *Dumbo*. Summarize the story of *Dumbo* for staff members: A baby elephant is born to Mrs. Jumbo, a circus elephant. The baby has enormous ears and is teased and called "Dumbo." His mother goes into a rampage trying to defend her baby and is locked away. Dumbo is left with his only friend, a mouse who uses a magic feather to convince the baby elephant to reach his full potential—to use his large ears to fly.

Give each staff member a feather and remind them that they, too, can fly this year. Incorporate the feather theme into awards and accomplishments throughout the year.

Work as a T—E—A—M and No Whining!

Set the expectation from the beginning that the goal for the year is to work together as a T-E-A-M (**T**ogether **E**veryone **A**chieves **M**ore). It is difficult to make a team out of a group of unique individuals. Just because everyone comes to the same school each day, wears the same school logo on their T-shirts, and shares the same mascot, that does not make them a team. You will need to practice being a team and helping each other achieve common goals.

One principle that will help the team process is *No Whining!* Often, there are toxic people in a workplace and a lot of nonproductive complaining goes on. I heard about a company that implemented a policy where employees could only complain to someone who had the knowledge or position to solve the problem. Violators would be terminated. So a person who had a problem with a colleague couldn't just randomly complain to other staff members.

Set the expectation that during the year, nonproductive complaining is to be avoided. Some people just need to get their feelings out, so create a place for staff members to *whine down*. You could call it the *Whine Cellar*. Put white boards or rolls of paper and markers for staff to vent their frustrations, and have erasers and wastebaskets on hand. Put stress-relieving toys in the room and have nice music available. (Make sure you don't make it nicer than the staff lounge or it may become the staff members' favorite hangout!) Make admission tickets for each staff member to have on hand. When a colleague starts complaining, give that person a ticket to the *Whine*

Cellar. You will be amazed at how much more productive staff members will be when there is not an undercurrent of gossip.

Make posters or banners with the following message. Post them in locations where staff members congregate, such as at the entrance of the building, or in the lounge, office, and so on.

T-E-A-M

If you work here, please do so with a positive attitude and a sense of humor.

If there is an issue to discuss, bring ideas for solutions. Do not discuss it with anyone who cannot solve the problem.

And...do not bad-mouth any members of our team.

We are just that...a TEAM.

Above and Beyond

Send a welcome-back letter to staff members, and in it, include a balloon and strip of paper. Ask each staff member to write a personal goal on the paper and insert it into the balloon. On the first day back, collect and fill the balloons with helium. Use them to decorate the meeting room. As part of the day's agenda, discuss the theme and plan events for the year. At the end of the day, have each staff member randomly select a balloon, pop it, and read the goal written inside. Post all of the goals in a common meeting place as a reminder of the group's plans to go above and beyond this year! *(Susan Saint John, Starlight Cove Elementary, Lantana, FL)*

Teeing Up Into the New School Year!

Sleepy Hollow Elementary School, in Sleepy Hollow, Illinois, used a golf theme to start their year. The principal sent out a welcome-back letter that used golf terms to announce the opening day staff meeting. The recipients were encouraged to wear golf attire.

Dear _____,

Greetings and welcome back for the new school year. Our faculty theme this year is the game of golf. So as you plan for the beginning of school, be certain to "tee up" for the new year.

Let's prepare to putt our way to victory as we play the Sleepy Hollow course. Please join us on the green Monday, August 21, 20___. For our first round together, we will meet on the fairway (a.k.a. gymnasium) at 8:00 a.m. for a continental breakfast. Our official tee time is set for 8:20 a.m. You can hit a hole in one by donning your favorite golf attire.

 Wishing you a *par*-fect year,

Anastasia

Principal

Plan an in-school golf game for staff members during the back-to-school inservice. Create five or more holes of various lengths that require participants to putt down the hallways, around cubicles, under desks, and around the trash can. Or transform an area such as the gym into a golf course.

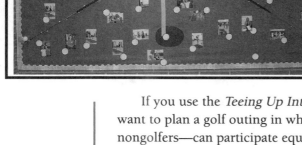

Take pictures of the staff members as they return to school during the summer to set up their rooms, and have a bulletin board prepared using these photos and the golf theme. (*Anastasia Epstein, Sleepy Hollow Elementary School, Sleepy Hollow, IL*)

If you use the *Teeing Up Into the New School Year* theme, you may want to plan a golf outing in which all staff members—golfers and nongolfers—can participate equally. For instance, play a round in which you may hit with only two clubs. Or give each person a string that is 36 inches long and a pair of scissors. The players may move their balls out of the woods, sand traps, and so on, but each time they do, they have to cut off a corresponding number of inches from their string. The winner is the person with the lowest score and the longest piece of string.

Follow the Yellow Brick Road to Success

Greet the staff dressed as a character from *The Wizard of Oz*—Dorothy, the Wizard, Tin Man, Lion, Scarecrow, and so on—and have the music from the movie playing over the PA system. Emphasize the need for a heart, courage, and a brain in order to be successful.

You Are the KEYS to Success

This could be the theme for the year or for a meeting with a Professional Learning Communities (PLC) team. The theme *You Are the KEYS* (**K**ids **E**xpect **Y**our **S**miles) *to Success* plays on the use of the word *keys*. Have the song "I've Got a Brand New Pair of Roller Skates" playing when the staff members arrive. At the end of the meeting, celebrate with key lime pie! *(Vicki Lewis, Washington Elementary School, Miami, OK)*

Rolling in a Great New Year!

Introduce the *Rolling in a Great New Year* theme by inviting faculty and staff members for dinner and a bowling night. Award fun prizes such as *Most Gutter Balls* and *Most Fabulous Form*. Beth Richert shared, "We laughed and celebrated good and bad bowling techniques." *(Beth Richert, Washington Elementary School, Clinton, OK)*

We Have the Thirst for Success!

Quench the staff members' thirst throughout the year by serving beverages for success. For the opening day of school, have a beverage bar waiting for them that is full of refreshing cold drinks.

At the start of the year, ask staff members to list their favorite beverages, and then keep their responses on file. Have a "hydration station" for staff members to visit as a recognition treat for a job well done or to visit during parent-teacher conferences.

Stock a beverage cart with the beverages the staff listed as their favorites. Visit each person's work area and deliver his or her beverage of choice.

When staff members are involved in team meetings, help them with the thirst for success. Stock a cart with iced tea and lemonade, and deliver beverages to each of the teams. Cover the cart with a tablecloth and flowers for an added touch. Make a sign to attach to the cart that reinforces the theme. *(Jarcelynn Hart, Rosa Parks Elementary School, Woodbridge, VA)*

Throughout the year, have staff members nominate their peers for a "beverage break." Select one staff member each week to receive the beverage of their choice, and include a note that explains why he or she was nominated.

We Have *GRAPE* Expectations

Use the *grape* theme throughout the year. Make purple the color of your opening day celebration, and decorate with purple balloons, banners, and crepe paper. When you send the back-to-school notice to staff, ask them to wear purple attire on their first day back. Serve refreshments such as sparkling grape juice and grape popsicles.

During the year, give staff members "You Are the Grapest" awards when they have noteworthy achievements. You could plan a "grape escape" and have either a staff outing or a grape juice and snacks event.

Welcome Back Gifts

Many districts have welcome back gifts for staff members as they begin the new school year. Typically, these are items that represent the school or can be used in the course of their jobs. Having the district's logo printed on the gift item is a good way to build school pride. Such items include a district T-shirt, memo cube, or writing portfolio. The following are some suggestions for low-cost or free items.

School Lanyards

Purchase commercially made lanyards for each staff member. Make them in your school's colors and embroider the school's name on them. Personalize each one by having the first and last name of each staff member embroidered onto the string. Staff members can attach their school identification badges or whistles onto them. *(Cher Lecours, Breeze Hill Elementary School, Vista, CA)*

Goodie Bags

Have area businesses donate items and use these in goodie bags that are waiting at each staff member's work station or at each seat at an all-staff breakfast. The items don't have to be expensive; they can be cute things, such as small first-aid kits, pencils, key chains, or fast food gift certificates.

Coupon Books

Give each staff member a coupon book with coupons that can be used throughout the year. Some coupons require advance notice and should be marked appropriately. Some examples of coupons include the following:

- Wear Jeans for a Day
- Leave Early
- Arrive Late
- One Dozen Cookies From the Cafeteria
- Free Cafeteria Lunch
- Free Car Wash
- Extended Lunch Time
- One Exemption From Lunch Duty
- One Exemption From Recess Duty

Card Them

Many people respond to seeing their names in print. Have business cards and personalized notepads made for all staff members—teachers, administrative assistants, food service workers, and the custodial and maintenance teams—*all* staff members. Then, for holiday or staff appreciation events,

VBISD
Van Buren Intermediate School District
Patti Kenworthy
Instructional Manager, Hospitality Services
Michigan Restaurant Association
Food Service Teacher of the Year

have personalized notepads printed. These are inexpensive and often can be printed by students enrolled in the district's technology program.

If staff members have received local, state, or national awards, be sure to include them on the card. This lets the staff member keep on being recognized.

Supplies Party

It's no secret that teachers spend a lot of their own money on classroom supplies. To help offset this expense, hold a *Welcome Back Supplies Party.* Ask parents, businesses, and vendors to provide supply items that staff members can select for their classes.

Variation 1

Fill plastic storage boxes with stickers and other supplies, and give one box to each teacher.

Variation 2

Give each person a coupon for a 50-dollar warehouse order to requisition classroom supplies. Attach a note to the order form that says, "The best resource in the school is you!" or "We are fortunate to have a supply of excellent staff members in our school."

Survival Kits

Make a survival kit for each staff member by placing the following instructions in a bag along with the items mentioned. You don't need to include all of the items; rather, select the ones you prefer. You could also give the staff a starter kit and add items to the kit each week as the year progresses.

If you don't want to assemble the survival kits yourself, Positive Promotions (www.positivepromotions.com) has Welcome Back Teachers and Staff Survival Kits and Welcome Back Teachers and Staff Snack Packs at very reasonable prices.

Survival Kits

Toothpick	To remind you to pick out the good qualities in others.
Rubber band	To remind you to be flexible throughout the day.
Paper clip	To remind you to hold it all together.
Eraser	To remind you to start each day with a clean slate.
Adhesive bandage	To remind you to heal hurt feelings—yours or others'.
Clay	To remind you that you are molding futures.
Life Savers	For always being there when others need you.
Marble	To replace the marbles we lose from time to time.
Mint	To remind you that you are worth a mint.
Tea bag	To remind you to relax and take time for yourself.
Pipe cleaner	Flexibility is important for a successful year.
Rick rack	This year will be full of ups and downs, but it will all smooth out.
Wiggly eye	To remind you to keep an eye on the students to determine how to best help them.
Battery	Like the Energizer Bunny, this will keep you going, and going, and going.
Animal cracker	For when you think your job is a zoo.
Jingle bell	Ring for help when you need it.
Present	To remind you that our students are a gift to us.
Candy bar	Use when you need a sweet escape.
Snowflake	When all else fails, hope for a Snow Day!
Flowerpot	We are here to plant the seeds of knowledge.
Clothespin	To remind you to hang in there.
Hole reinforcers	Don't forget to reinforce each other's efforts.

Thought for the Week

Type inspiring, motivational quotes from books such as *Quote This!* (see www.corwin.com) on small strips of colored paper. Put them in a ribbon-decorated jar. At the start of the year, give each staff member a jar for his or her desk. On Monday, have staff members select a quote from their jars to reflect on for the week. You will need to vary the quotes for instructional and noninstructional staff. Here is a starter list:

There is no word in the language I revere more than "teacher." My heart sings when a kid refers to me as his teacher, and it always has. I've honored myself and the entire family of man by becoming a teacher.

—Pat Conroy

We could all learn a lot from crayons:
Some are sharp,
Some are pretty,
Some are dull,
Some have weird names,
And all are different colors . . .
But they all have learned to live in the same box.

—Unknown

Bloom where you are planted.

—Mary Englebreit

Always put yourself in others' shoes. If you feel it hurts, it will probably hurt the other person, too.

—Unknown

I have seen what a laugh can do. It can transform almost unbearable tears into something bearable, even hopeful.

—Bob Hope

> We shall never know all the good that a simple smile can do.
>
> —Mother Teresa
>
> We should know that we are all part of the whole, we are all together. And everything that we do affects each other.
>
> —Yoko Ono

WELCOMING NEW STAFF MEMBERS

Starting a new job is both exhilarating and challenging. Make the experience a joyful one by implementing some of these welcoming activities. Make sure the work area is ready for a new person—nothing says *welcome* more than evidence of preparation.

Staff E-mails

Prior to the start of the new school year, send an e-mail to all returning staff members. In it, include a picture and bio of each new staff member. This will allow team members to identify things they have in common with the new staff and will help them engage in conversation when they meet.

Eat and Greet

Hold an informal *Eat and Greet* in which staff members are served snacks and meet new staff members. Some favorite fun foods include the following:

- Cookies
- Pizza
- Donuts

- Bagels
- Fruit
- Ice cream
- Popcorn
- Candy
- Salty snacks
- Potato chips
- Pretzels

Hi Tea

Host a *Hi Tea* with tea, finger sandwiches, and cookies to introduce new staff members to the veterans. Obtain a variety of types of tea cups

from a discount store. Allow the staff members to individually select a cup, and let them keep it at the end of the event.

Another variation is to ask each person to bring a tea cup to share. Each staff member tells why the cup was selected and how it relates to something in his or her life, and then gives it to another staff member to take home. You may also want to encourage staff members to wear hats for the occasion.

Banners and Bows

Have welcome banners and pictures displayed at the entrance of the school. On the first day of school, give new staff members a bow or flower to wear or carry to show that they are new to the school.

Welcome Packets

Give new staff members a welcome packet of items with the school's logo on them, such as a pin, pen, or sweatshirt. In addition, give them a coffee mug with the district's mission statement printed on it. Also, include a book of educational humor such as *Laugh Lines for Educators* (www.corwin.com); they will need it.

Names in Lights!

Have an electronic message displayed on the sign board that welcomes the new staff by name. Ask area businesses to also put the names on the message boards in front of their buildings.

New Staff Member Toast

Welcome the new staff members with *toast* (yes, real toast). Serve nonalcoholic sparking juice in champagne glasses and prepare toast with assorted jams and jellies. Toast the success of the new staff members and welcome them to your school.

New Staff Member Shower

Hold a shower for new staff members. Give each staff member a large plastic bag. (They won't have any idea what it is to be used for.) Have other staff members give them gifts that can be used in their classrooms, such as bulletin board displays, a card file of ideas, classroom management gifts, and lesson plans. Not only are the items useful, they will also help the new staff members feel welcomed by their colleagues. They will be talking about this event throughout the year.

Pancake Year

Meet with the new staff members and let them know that this is their *Pancake Year.* Explain that when you make pancakes, the first one isn't really quite right. The shape is a bit off, and the temperature might be wrong. The first pancake goes on the bottom of the pile, and the rest get better. Decorate a pancake turner, and give it to the group. Encourage the new members to get together periodically to share what has gone well and what needs to improve. At the end of the year, the group votes on who gets to keep the pancake turner—either for the most successful new member or the one who had the most memorable experience. That person then passes the pancake turner on to next year's new group of staff members.

Community Welcome

Often, community organizations assist in welcoming new staff members. In Lake Havasu City, Arizona, the Chamber of Commerce hosted a mixer at an area resort and invited all the new teachers from the district for the past two years and their mentors, school board members, and administrators. The new teachers received a variety of donated gifts from the chamber businesses. Appetizers and other refreshments were served throughout the evening and underwritten by the resort.

Other community businesses have adopted new staff members. Each business adopts a teacher for a period of three years. When the teachers need outside resources or assistance of any kind, they ask their community mentor, who is networked with other community resources. It's nice to have a team of mentors and to feel welcomed by the community in which you work.

CHAPTER 3

Fabulous Fall

September Through November

PAUSE FOR APPLAUSE

Advanced Planning Reward

Vacation

It is often difficult for staff members to travel during holiday breaks. Before the start of the school year, ask parents if they would donate enough frequent flier miles to send two people (the staff member and a guest) on a trip. Determine how staff members become eligible for the drawing. For example, each week or month the person has perfect attendance, his or her name is entered; each person serving on a school committee is entered; or those who turn grades in on time are entered. Be sure to hold the drawing well in advance of the vacation period so that the winner can plan the travel and make sure airline seats are available.

Going Above and Beyond

Apple Awards

Variation 1

Give this award twice each year to employees who have contributed beyond what is considered to be their jobs. Award winners are selected by the superintendent, principals, or directors. The recipients receive a red apple pin and are featured in a newsletter article.

Variation 2

After Christmas is a great time to buy apple ornaments because they are on sale. Write "Thanks" on them with a paint marker. When a staff member does something notable, give him or her a red apple. *(Karen Doyle, Congetta Trippe Janet Elementary School, Marrero, LA)*

Variation 3

The Golden Apple Award is given each month at a faculty meeting to people who have gone above and beyond their job responsibilities. The actual award is a gold-colored apple mounted on a wooden base. In September, the principal selects the recipient and makes the award presentation to that employee. That person then selects the recipient

> Do more than you are paid for. There are never any traffic jams on the extra mile.
>
> —*Brian Tracy*

for the month of October, and so it goes for the rest of the year. The person passing the award on gives a brief presentation as to why the new recipient was selected. In the office, there is a plaque for each school year engraved with the name of each month's recipient. *(Liz Vaden, Eastern Alamance High School, Mebane, NC)*

You Deserve a Gold Medal

When designing your school newsletter, make a "You Deserve a Gold Medal" section. In it, recognize staff members who have gone above and beyond in helping students, colleagues, or the school. *(Cheryl Zigrang, Thoroughgood Elementary School, Virginia Beach, VA)* You could also award gold medals to recipients à la the Olympics.

Sunshine Awards

Awards are given by administrators to staff members for helping a coworker or going above and beyond. The recommendations for the award may be made by administrators or staff members. Sunshine pins are presented to the recipients at the monthly staff meetings. The key is to make sure that all staff members are recognized at least once each year. *(Ginny Griffin, City of Medicine Academy, Durham, NC)*

Community Service Award

Service is nothing but love in work clothes.

—*Unknown*

Present a plaque to a staff member for outstanding contributions in the area of community-school relations.

Professional Development Award

Recognize people who have made an extra effort in the area of their own professional development. Likely, this award will need to be given for education not paid for by the school.

Student Activities Award

Many staff members take on the responsibility for student activities for which they receive no compensation. Give an award to those who demonstrate this commitment to students.

Awards for Goal Achievement

Mission Accomplished or Mission Possible Award

Create an award that can be given to either individual staff members or teams for achieving a goal. Give the award a fun name that also reflects its intent. It could be the Mission Possible Award or the Mission Accomplished Award. If you use the *Mission Possible* theme, incorporate the theme song from the movie *Mission Impossible* into your presentation. Staff members can nominate colleagues or themselves for these awards. You may want to establish a review committee who selects the recipient. Celebrate success with a fun event!

Mortgage Shredding Party

Setting a goal and then reaching it is deserving of celebration! If your district has a monumental event such as paying off a construction bond, hold a bond shredding party. (This is much safer than having a bond burning party!) Invite all district staff and Board of Education members to attend this ceremonial event. Have refreshments and a door prize to make the event even more special. *(Debby Sharp, Bridgeport School District, Bridgeport, WA)*

Pop a Balloon—Receive a Prize

Determine which achievements you want to celebrate and reward during the year: for example, attendance, a predetermined percentage of parental participation in Back to School Night, fundraising success, or submitting grades on time.

Create a bulletin board (cork works best) that's designated as the reward board. (Put this in a safe place where there is no student access because darts will be used.) Put a slip of paper that lists a prize (reward) on it into a large quantity of balloons. The rewards could be coupons for an early release day, free lunch from the cafeteria, a restaurant coupon, a gift donated by a vendor, classroom supplies, an extended lunch break, and so on.

When a person reaches a goal, he or she is given a dart and gets one try to pop a balloon. The prize listed on the paper inside the balloon is then awarded to that person. If he or she fails to pop a balloon, no prize is awarded. You  will also have to decide what to do if multiple balloons are popped. (It's easy to pop a cluster of balloons, and sometimes the dart pops other balloons when it falls to the ground.) Does the person receive all of the prizes, or does he or she get to select the prize of his or her choice from the balloons that are popped? Do any of the balloons contain papers that say "Thank you. Try again"? (Warning: You may find that people start to practice their dart throwing!)

General Recognition

Teacher of the Month

Create a form on which students and parents list the reasons why a certain teacher deserves to be honored. Ask community businesses to donate gift cards to be given to the teachers. Send a picture and an article to the local newspaper to announce your school's Teacher of the Month. "The teachers really enjoy reading the comments by students and parents more than the gift card." *(Karen Doyle, Congetta Trippe Janet Elementary School, Marrero, LA)*

Heroes

Let the staff members know they are heroes. Make a banner that says, "Every Day You Have the Chance to Be a Hero to a Student." Hang it in a place staff members frequent, such as the mailroom.

Have the principal create an area in the office that says, "Heroes That I Get to Work for Every Day," and display photos of the staff members.

Collect staff member information on a survey sheet such as the one on the next page. With the information, create a Hero of the Week publication that highlights information about each staff member. *(Tom Sharp, Oglethorpe County High School, Lexington, GA)*

Recognition is the greatest motivator.

—*Gerard C. Eakedale*

Hero of the Week

You have been selected as a Hero of the Week. Please provide information about yourself and e-mail it back to me by the end of the week. This information will be shared with other staff members as a way for all of us to get to know each other better. Provide only the information you want shared with your colleagues.

Name:

Place of birth:

Day and month (only) of birthday:

Places where you have lived:

Number of brothers:

Where do they live?

Number of sisters:

Where do they live?

Names and ages of children:

Did you work before you graduated from high school? If so, doing what?

Jobs you had during and after college:

Hobbies:

Favorite food(s):

Favorite vehicle you have owned:

Talent that others might not know you have:

Favorite vacation spot:

The thing you love most about working at (name of school):

Fantastic Friday Assemblies (FFA)

On Friday mornings, hold Fantastic Friday Assemblies for staff and students. Give out fun Golden Awards, such as the Golden Elephant Award, to the class that did the best job in remembering their reading books. This is a time to recognize the accomplishments of the staff and students and to celebrate (and sing to) those who have birthdays that week. "We love our FFAs . . . and our attendance on Fridays is way up." *(Marcy Aycock, Prairie Elementary School, Haysville, KS)*

A Sporting Recognition

Implement this recognition activity throughout the year when there are home sporting events. Have sports teams select a school employee to be recognized as Staff Member of the Week. The person who is the recipient of the award receives free admission to the event and a concession stand gift certificate, is recognized by the sports announcer, and is applauded by the crowd. Bringing the staff member onto the field, court, or track to receive recognition is even more meaningful. *(Tom Sharp, Oglethorpe County High School, Lexington, GA)*

POPs Awards

Establish POPs Awards (Power of the Positive) for the staff (and students). Hold assemblies to recognize people for acts of kindness, attendance, and so on. *(Robin Frost, Conestoga District, Murray, NE)* Wouldn't it be great if each award winner received a Power of the Positive T-shirt that could be worn on casual day or at future assemblies? This will help show how many recipients there have been each year.

Friday Fan E-mail

Each time a staff member receives praise or recognition from a coworker, parent, community member, and so on, it is forwarded to a designated person (typically the school's administrative assistant or someone in Human Resources). Compile these recognitions into an e-mail and, each Friday, send it to all staff members in the school or district. Once a month, hold a drawing from the names that were submitted, and give the winner a gift certificate or other prize.

Kindness Jars

Have the staff read *How Full Is Your Bucket?* by Tom Rath and Donald O. Clifton. This book is based on the concept that each of us has an

> There is more hunger for love and appreciation in this world than for bread.
>
> —Mother Teresa

> Ask someone else how he knows when he has done a good job. For some people, the proof comes from outside. The boss pats you on the back and says your work was great . . . you win a big award. Your work is noticed and applauded by your peers.
>
> —Tony Robbins

invisible bucket. This bucket is always in the process of being emptied or filled, depending on how we are treated and how we treat others. When the bucket is full, we feel wonderful and fulfilled. However, when it is empty, we feel empty as well.

In addition, we all come with an invisible dipper that we can use to fill the buckets of others. This can be done by saying or doing nice things that elicit positive feelings. We can fill our own buckets the same way. Conversely, the dipper can be used to dip from buckets by doing and saying things that make us and others feel bad.

When the bucket is full, we are energized, fulfilled, positive. Likewise, when it is empty, our energy level drops, our outlook is clouded, and we don't feel good about ourselves.

Each day we are faced with a choice—to fill or dip from each other's buckets. It is a choice that influences relationships, health, and careers, among other things.

Give each staff member an empty jar and a supply of glass marbles in a small bag. Each time they do something nice for someone else, they add a marble to the jar. Likewise, when there is negativity, they have to remove a marble and put it back in their bag. Ask the staff members to keep the jars in view so they have a daily reminder about the choices they make.

Variation

Use this concept and apply it to reaching the school's goals. Give each grade level a supply of glass marbles, which represent drops of water (and steps toward achieving the school's goals), and a glass jar, which represents a bucket. Have each grade level meet as a group and review the action steps necessary to achieve the school's goals. As each action step is completed, have them drop a glass marble into the grade-level bucket. This will assist teachers in realizing their success in reaching their grade-level goals for the year. *(Wendy Ricci, Horizon Elementary School, Madison, AL)*

Breakfast of Champions

Sponsor a staff breakfast called *Breakfast of Champions* after a special event, such as standardized testing, parent-teacher conferences, or a sporting event. It can be either a potluck or a meal that is provided for the staff. You could also ask the community to sponsor some of the food items and note the contributions on the buffet line.

Champions Billboard

Ask sign companies to donate unused billboard space. Create a champions billboard that features the pictures of staff members. Let each employee group select the person(s) who will be featured.

Gift Card Drawing

Ask local businesses to donate 10-dollar gift cards for staff members. Put each card in an individual, unmarked envelope. Have staff members select an envelope to discover the prize and find out which business is providing the gift. *(Eric Dennis, Conestoga Elementary School, Murray, NE)*

Sweet Rewards

Food is a great reward for staff members, and a great time to buy candy on sale is right after Halloween. Stock up on some of the items listed on the next page, and when the time is right, attach an appreciative saying to the candy and distribute the treats at staff meetings, put them on staff members' desks, or drop them in teachers' mailboxes. You could also give out one item a day during annual testing weeks. Some examples of candy rewards include:

Dove Promises—Thanks for giving your *promise* to help students learn.

Starbursts—You are a *star bursting* with enthusiasm.

Our students' test *SKOR*s are great. Thanks for your efforts.

SKOR—Our students' test *SKOR*s are great. Thanks for your efforts!

Bites—You take the *bite* out of coming to work.

Red Hots—Our staff is *red hot!*

M & M's—*Marvelous & Motivated*—That's You! You *mean* so *much* to our students!

Nestlé Treasures—We *treasure* the work you do! Having you on staff is a real *treasure.*

100 Grand won't suffice for the *100 Grand* things that you do.

100 Grand—*100 Grand* won't suffice for the *100 Grand* things that you do.

Gummi Bears—We are *beary* glad you are a part of our staff!

Hugs—*Huge Undertaking! Great Success!* Thanks for *Helping Us Give to Students!*

SweeTARTS—You are such a *SweeTART!* Thanks for the help!

Pixie Stix—Your skill as a teacher really *stix* out!

PayDay—An extra *PayDay* for all of your efforts!

Life Savers—Thanks for being a *Life Saver!*

Riesen—You are one of the *riesens* our students succeed!

Tootsie Roll—Thank you for the *roll* you play in our students' success.

You comple-*mint* our staff so well!

Mint—You were *mint* to be a teacher. You comple-*mint* our staff so well! You are worth a *mint* to us! Thank you for your commit-*mint* to our students.

Any kind of candy—Working with you is a *sweet treat!*

64 Season It With Fun!

Rewards of Time

G.O.O.S.E. Award

G.O.O.S.E. stands for *get out of school early.* These early release awards are given to staff members so that they can leave ahead of schedule. An administrator covers the classroom for 15 minutes before dismissal so that the award winner can depart early. *(Karen Doyle, Congetta Trippe Janet Elementary School, Marrero, LA)*

Get Out of a Duty FREE Card

Give the staff member a small, business-type card that reads something like the one on the right.

The principal gives staff members a break by covering a duty for each person. *(Sandi Morris, Edmonton Public Schools, Alberta, Canada)*

Get out of a duty...FREE

John Connor
The Principal

This card entitles you to a break. I will cover one of your duties at a pre-arranged time.

Stand in Their Shoes

Give the staff members a coupon for the principal to teach in each teacher's classroom for a half-day each year. The teachers may remain on campus to do school-related work or they may use it as personal time off campus. This allows the staff members to have some discretionary time and the principal to hone his or her teaching skills and be a "teaching principal." *(Tami Shelley, Trinity Presbyterian School, Montgomery, AL)*

Attendance Rewards

Tie a Colored Ribbon

Post a ribbon or bow in the school colors outside the classroom of any teacher who has perfect attendance for the week or marking period.

Attendance Lottery

Set up a lottery with large gifts—for example, a weekend at a hotel, dinner for two at an area restaurant, theater tickets, or a discretionary day off from work—to be awarded at the end of each marking period. Set up the criteria that best fits your school or district, such as perfect, or very good, attendance. Those who qualify are given a ticket. At the end of each marking period, hold a drawing to select the winner of the prize. You may also want to hold a drawing at the end of the year for those who had perfect attendance throughout.

Basket of Goodies Drawing

Each month, prepare, or have the community donate, a basket of goodies that relates to either the season or a holiday appropriate for that month. Staff members who have perfect attendance for the month are eligible for the drawing. The winner receives the basket of goodies. (*Karen Doyle, Jefferson Parish, Marrero, LA*)

Jeans Pass

Each month, give staff members with the best attendance two passes that allow them to wear jeans to work. Make stickers or buttons for staff members to wear with their jeans that say, "I Have Great Attendance and Earned This Jeans Day."

Parking Space Drawing

Put the names of staff members who have perfect attendance for the week in a container for a drawing. The person whose name is drawn gets

the parking space of his or her choice for the week. Hold the drawing at the weekly staff meeting or on Monday morning, and share the winner's name during the daily announcements. Make a sign designating the winner's special spot. (This drawing could instead be done on a monthly basis or at the end of each marking period.)

Saying Thank You

Saying thank you is one of the most basic ways of showing appreciation. We all know we can do it, but ask yourself, "Am I doing it?" Here are some ways to express thanks.

Thank-You Cards Drawing

Make thank-you cards that have two sections and distribute them to all staff members. Half of the card features the message of thanks. The other half is detachable and has room for the person's name and contact information. That portion of the note is submitted for a drawing each marking period; winners receive a gift card, gas card, time-off coupon, some classroom supplies, and so on.

THANKS FOR THE GREAT EFFORT!

Report Card

DRAWING ENTRY

NAME:_____

CONTACT INFORMATION:_____

PLACE IN THE CONTAINER IN THE OFFICE FOR A
DRAWING AT THE END OF THE MARKING PERIOD.

Thanks a Million (or More)

To give thanks to a staff member, make a lottery ticket card. Size it to
be slightly larger than an actual lottery ticket and inscribe it with
Thanks a Million or *Thanks a* _____ (the amount of the
current lottery jackpot, for example, 23 million) *for* _____.
Be sure to indicate the specific behavior you are rewarding. *(Kathi
Breweur, Chapel Hill-Carrboro City Schools, Chapel Hill, NC)*

> Feeling gratitude and not expressing it is like wrapping a present and not giving it.
>
> —William Arthur Ward

Handwritten Notes

Make a commitment to write a note to every staff person at least once a year. (*Patrick O'Neil, Aiken County Career and Technology Center, Warrenville, SC*)

Peer Recognition

Pass It Along

Select an item that will be passed around among the staff members. "Our school mascot is the roadrunner. Over the summer I found a metal roadrunner lawn decoration at a farmers market. I presented the Roving Roadrunner Award at the first staff meeting to a staff member who made a positive contribution. That person kept the award until the next week, when she presented it to another colleague and wrote the reason for choosing the new recipient in the weekly staff bulletin. The Roving Roadrunner Award has been traveling throughout the school from staff member to staff member, including teachers, office staff, food service personnel, custodians, and paraprofessionals. This is a great recognition from colleague to colleague for things to which I am not always privy."

You can use any type of award that fits your school—and it just keeps going and going. (*Mark French, Rice Lake Elementary School, Maple Grove, MN*)

Super Staff Bulletin Board

Randomly select a staff person to be the super staff person for the month. Put a picture of the staff member on a bulletin board display. Give staff members blank yellow stars and ask them to write a positive statement about the person being featured. Place the stars on the bulletin board for all to read. (*Jessica Perone, Neighborhood Centers of Johnson County, Iowa City, IA*)

> It is important that you recognize your progress and take pride in your accomplishments. Share your achievements with others. Brag a little. The recognition and support of those around you is nurturing.
>
> —Rosemarie Rossetti

Put It on the Intranet

Create kudos bulletin boards as part of the district's intranet system. Staff members can post praise for their colleagues on this site so that when staff members log on to their computers, everyone can read them. You will need someone to manage the bulletin boards so that old messages are deleted to make room for new ones. This is a great way to highlight innovative ideas that have been successful and to praise the efforts of those who made it happen.

Every week I send out an electronic newsletter to the staff called *The Firebird File*—Firebirds are our mascot. Page 2 of the newsletter is called "The Braggin' Wall," where we share our successes each week. A sentence or two about a noteworthy achievement can be sent in by any staff for inclusion on this page.

Cost: $0

Feedback: Very positive

Impact: Priceless

(Ed West, Free State High School, Lawrence, KS)

Unexpected Acts of Kindness

It feels good to just do something nice for someone. I travel a lot and spend hours in airports. I keep a supply of coffee shop gift cards in my purse to give to military personnel standing in line for coffee. One time I approached a young soldier and tried to give him the card. He said he couldn't take it because he was "just doing his job." I told him my father was an Army colonel and would be pleased if he accepted the gift card. The young man responded, "Yes, ma'am," and took the card.

Leave anonymous notes with positive comments for staff members. They will feel good and wonder who the note was from.

SPC Committee

Form a Special People Care (SPC) Committee whose mission is to help others when they need it most. The members of the committee remain anonymous. Money is collected so that when staff members have a death in the family, an illness, or any other unfortunate incident, the committee can help them.

POWERED BY FUN!

The End-of-the-Year Advanced Preparation

Give each person a disposable camera and ask them to take pictures of events that happen during the year. At the end of the year, make a compilation of these photos using a scrapbook, DVD, or bulletin board.

Fun Grants

Create *Fun Grants*. A person, group, or committee can submit ideas for ways to bring fun and enjoyment to the school. The grants can be used for events such as an ice cream social or hot chocolate day.

A child came home from his first day at school.

His mother asked, "Well, what did you learn today?"

The kid replied, "Not enough. They want me to come back tomorrow."

I appointed a fun committee! They have candy, games, and prizes at each staff meeting. There is a token award that gets passed to the winning team each time. We all get a laugh and work together! All I gave them was the book *Looking Forward to Monday Morning* and a small budget. There has been excitement and laughter each time.

(Nancy Moga, Callaghan Elementary School, Covington, VA)

Payday Play

Make paydays even more special. One principal reported that she dresses up every payday and delivers the paychecks to each staff member. She has been known to put dollar bills all over her body or to dress up like a turkey in November. (That's the only time that staff members are allowed to call her a turkey!)

Another principal gave each staff member a pay bonus: 100 Grand (the candy bar, of course)! On it he attached a note that said, "You are worth $100 Grand, but this is all I can afford."

Others have reported giving their colleagues a PayDay candy bar on a non-payday Friday, so they had an extra payday that month. *(Tami Barrett, Hugh Bish Elementary School, Lawton, OK)*

Football Celebrations

Football season brings many opportunities for fun activities. Here are a few you might implement in your school.

T-shirt or Sweatshirt Day—All staff members are encouraged to wear a T-shirt or sweatshirt that supports either a favorite professional or college football team or the college or university they graduated from.

Rival Team Fun—Colleges and universities have rivalries with other schools, and this makes the competition even more exciting. For example, Ohio State University (OSU) and the University of Michigan (U of M) are rival universities. Staff members had fun when these teams played each other.

Staff members who wore OSU attire on the Friday before the game had their names entered into a contest. At the end of the day, names were selected as prize winners. The winners received a framed photo of Brutus Buckeye, a framed photo of the OSU stadium, or cheerleader pom-poms. Darlene Roll shared, "There were many cries of 'Pick me, pick me!' coming from the staff during the drawing."

Those who dared to wear the maize and blue of U of M were given M&Ms for Michigan madness. *(Darlene Roll, Ohio High-Point Career Center, Bellefontaine, OH)*

Social Board

Hang a whiteboard where staff members can post notices about upcoming social events that are happening in the community—a new movie, sports event, and so on. The person who lists the event becomes the organizer and staff members can sign up to participate.

Q and A

Put a whiteboard in a location where staff members congregate. Each week, or periodically throughout the year, write a question on the board. Staff members can respond and initial their responses. Some examples are shown.

If you had not gone into education, what career would you have pursued?

Miss Dee on Romper Room television show (DH)

Military (TG)

Sales (GM)

Whether you have the talent/ability, if you could do anything for a career and be successful, what would you do?

Pairs ice skater (DH)

Country singer (PK)

Bartender at Cheers (JD)

As a child, what was your favorite game?

Jacks (DH)

Jump rope (JT)

What is your pet peeve?

People who are always late (DH)

Negative people (CW)

Multitasking while driving (DS)

People who don't use their turn signals when changing lanes (FD)

Mad Hatter Day

Mad Hatter Day is celebrated on October 6th. The Hatter is a fictional character from *Alice's Adventures in Wonderland*, by Lewis Carroll. Alice came across him at a tea party. He is never called by name in the book, but is generally referred to as *the Mad Hatter* because of his eccentric behavior.

Encourage staff members (and students) to wear creative hats to school. Judging the hats is optional, and prizes can be awarded for the craziest, most creative, most lovely, most team spirited, and so on.

Variation

Host a Mad Hatter Tea Party. To be admitted, you must wear a hat.

Snow Day Contest

If you live in a place where it snows, you know the mixed feelings that are generated by having the schools close because of weather. While some are chanting, "Snow day!" and waiting for the fan-out call list to be implemented so they can go back to bed, others are dreading the disruption it causes. In anticipation of this winter event, sponsor a Snow Day contest. To get people in the mood, have the staff sing the snow day song on page 74.

Tell staff members you are going to place a winter calendar where they congregate at work. Ask each person to pick a day he or she thinks will be the first Snow Day. Allow three names per day. The first person's name on a given day receives the first-place prize; the second name, second-place prize; and so on. Designate a blank square on the calendar for the selection of a "No Snow Day." If the last selected calendar day passes before there is a Snow Day, the people who picked the "No Snow Day" option are the winners. To add to the suspense, cross off each day that goes by without a Snow Day. The winner receives prizes such as the following:

First Place: An adjustable snow shovel with a matching ice scraper and brush

Second Place: Purple flying saucer and hand warmers

Snow Day

To the tune of "In the Ghetto" by Elvis Presley

Something's not right
I'm lyin' in a bed on a cold winter night
Something's scrapin' on the street so I turn
on the light
It's the snow plow

I put my boots on
I throw on my coat and go outside
By now the snow's half up to my thighs
We're gonna have a Snow Day

It's time to work the plan
I said with phone in hand
Speed dial's programmed for this holiday
I know just what to say
I rehearse it every day
It's a media event
We need it so
So stay inside and let it blow

Now the word's out
By now the phone's ringing off the wall
Just in case it was a prank phone call
It's a Snow Day

And the parents cry
The kids are gonna be home all day
They're gonna wanna eat
They're gonna wanna play
It's a Snow Day

Then in the middle of the afternoon
You finally get to check out the school
The halls are empty
So you get some work done
You check the weather
This is no fun

You look outside in the bright sunlight
There's a big snowman and a snowball fight
It's a Snow Day

No more snow plow
The snow has stopped
The streets are clear
Tomorrow they'll all be right back here
On a school day

Terry Doyle, Henderson, NV

Third Place: A gallon of windshield washer
fluid and bag of Ice Melt

*(Debra Macklin, Jennings Elementary School,
Quincy, MI)*

If you want to use this as a FUNdraising activity, have the staff
members purchase each square.

Odd Days

Mark your calendars now for 7/9/11, 9/11/13, and 11/13/15. Three
consecutive odd numbers make up the date only six times in a century,
and three of them have already taken place (1/3/5, 3/5/7, and 5/7/9).
Note that this only works in countries where the dates are written in
the sequence of month/date/year. How can you celebrate odd day?
Wear odd clothes and dress like odd characters. When those three
dates have passed, there won't be another odd day for 90 more years!
For more ideas visit www.oddday.net.

LOL

Ask every staff member to submit jokes for each school day. You will need
to divide the number of school days by the number of staff members to
determine how many jokes each person needs to submit. And emphasize
that the jokes need to be in good taste—no dumb blonde jokes, ethnic
humor, and so on. The joke of the day can appear in the daily
announcements, be posted in the lounge, sent as an e-mail, posted on the
bulletin board, and so on. If you are stumped for jokes, *Laugh Lines for
Educators* and *Grin and Share It!* (www.corwin.com) are filled with humor
related to education, children, teaching, and special occasions.

Kindergarten Gifts

It was the end of the school year, and the kindergarten teacher was receiving gifts from
her students.

The florist's son handed her a gift. She shook it, held it overhead, and said, "I bet I
know what it is. Is it flowers?"

"That's right," the boy said, "but how did you know?"

"Oh, just a wild guess," she replied.

(Continued)

(Continued)

The next student was the daughter of a candy shop owner. The teacher held the gift overhead, shook it, and said, "I bet I can guess what this is. Is it a box of candy?"

"That's right, but how did you know?" asked the girl.

"Oh, just another wild guess," said the teacher.

The next gift was from the son of a liquor store owner. The teacher held the gift overhead and noticed that it was leaking. She touched a drop of the liquid to her finger and then touched it with her tongue.

"Is it wine?" she asked.

"No," the boy replied with excitement.

The teacher repeated the process, taking a larger drop of the leakage to her tongue.

"Is it champagne?" she asked.

"No," the boy replied with excitement.

The teacher took one more taste before declaring, "I give up. What is it?"

With glee the boy replied, "It's a puppy!"

Source: Hodges, D. (2005). *Laugh lines for educators.* Thousand Oaks, CA: Corwin, p. 45.

50th Day of School

On the 50th day of school, hold a 1950s celebration. Have the staff and the students dress up in 1950s outfits. Many of the staff members were not born in that decade, so here are some dressing tips. Most people associate that period's style with Sandy and Danny from the movie and play *Grease*. The "greaser" guys wore jeans, white T-shirts, and leather jackets. They combed their hair back from their faces and then created a part down the back of their heads using the end of a comb, creating a hairstyle called *the ducktail*. Flat tops or crew cuts were also popular.

The girls wore either full skirts with petticoats or skirts that were narrow and straight. Poodle skirts were all the rage. The hemlines were usually below the knee—mid-calf. Blouses had small collars (called *Peter Pan collars*), and scarves tied around the neck were in. Wide belts were popular; they made the waistlines look smaller. When girls wore pants, they were usually mid-calf peddle pushers or Bermuda shorts that were knee length. Keds (canvas shoes) were worn with them. Hair styles were large and bouffant and required a lot of hairspray.

To create the ambience of the decade, play 1950s music such as "Rock Around the Clock," "Blue Suede Shoes," and "Mack the Knife," or hold a sing-along. You could also play "Name That Tune" with 1950s music or have a dance contest. You could show some of the television programs that were popular at the time, such as *I Love Lucy*, *The Honeymooners*, and *American Bandstand*. Another idea is to play 1950s trivia with the staff members. To add to the fun, have hula hoops available and see who is successful at keeping them going the longest.

When you send out the invitation for this event, you might want to use some of the words—the lingo—from the 1950s:

Bash—great party

Big Daddy—an older person

Blast—a good time

Bread—money

Bug—to bother

Cook or cookin'—doing well

Cool—someone who is extraordinary

Dibs—make a claim (I have dibs on the front seat.)

Don't have a cow—don't get upset

Flick—movie

Flip—to get very excited

Frosted—angry

Grody—sloppy, messy, dirty

(Continued)

(Continued)

Hep—someone who knows the situation

Hip—someone who is cool, in the know

Horn—telephone

Made in the shade—successful

Later—goodbye

Pad—home

Paper shaker—cheerleader

Peepers—glasses

Righto—OK

Sides—vinyl records

Split—leave

That's close—something that is wrong or untrue

Threads—clothes

Tight—good friends

Unreal—exceptional

Weed—a cigarette

What's buzzin,' Cuzzin?—What's new?

Paycheck With a Smile

On payday, put a comic or joke in staff members' pay envelopes. It adds a special surprise to each person's day. Do you want to make a random person's day? When you mail in your payment with your bills, put a fun comic in the envelope. It will give the person opening your envelope a fun moment.

Safari

Staff members from Gentiva Health Services, Kalamazoo, MI

Collect stuffed animals from garage sales or thrift stores, or ask parents to bring them in. Give each staff member an animal.

Have staff members determine an accomplishment that they want to achieve collectively. For example, an Open House might be approaching, and the staff members could set the goal to have 75% or higher parent participation in each classroom. When each staff member achieves that goal, he or she delivers the stuffed animal to the principal or other designated person. *How* the animal is delivered is the key. This is where the person's creativity comes into play. The animal could be gift wrapped, served on a silver platter, incorporated into a skit at a staff meeting, delivered over a door using a fishing hook and rod, dressed in the school colors, and so on. Have a fun time!

Lunch *Moments*

One of my friends is a third-grade teacher in California. As we were discussing this book, I was sharing ideas that staff members could use during their lunch periods. She corrected me and said they are lunch *moments.* Some of these activities require more than a moment to implement, but maybe if they were on the schedule, time could be made. (I do remember the 22-minute lunch period I was assigned at the middle school level.)

Theme Lunch Mondays

People often have food specialties they love to prepare (for example, breads, appetizers, salads, or desserts). Create a calendar for the year and designate the Monday after each payday as a Theme Lunch Day. If you have a large staff, people may sign up for a theme day (or two) when they would like to bring in something to share. Theme days could include the following:

- Ethnic foods
- Crockpot cuisine
- Salads
- Creative sandwiches
- Appetizers
- Desserts
- Soups
- Chef's choice

Each participant should provide copies of the recipes, which might be compiled into a staff cookbook.

Fun Friday/First Wednesday

You will need to start this event in the fall, but it is an activity that can be carried out throughout the year. Ask staff members to volunteer and form three or four committees. Each committee hosts a theme lunch for the staff members, including providing the decorations, music, and food. It is also nice to invite the central office staff members to join in the festivities. A theme could be *This Spud's for You*, and you could serve a baked potato bar. Or you could use the theme *It's 5 O'clock Somewhere* and serve Mexican food and nonalcoholic margaritas. Of course, you will want to either have Alan Jackson and Jimmy Buffett's song, "It's Five O'clock Somewhere," playing or show the video of them performing the song. *(Dana Oatley, J. E. Rhodes Primary School, Van, TX)*

Designate one day at the beginning of the month, such as First Wednesday, in which staff members sign up to bring or prepare lunch for all staff members. "Everyone really looks forward to this treat." *(Deborah Shelton, Big Island Elementary School, Big Island, VA)*

Staff Beverage Break

For the first three months of school, supply hot beverages for staff members in the break room. Provide gourmet coffee and tea with all of the fixings. Purchase decorative baskets to hold a variety of flavors of hot chocolate mixes and hot cider packets. Provide sweeteners, non-dairy creamers, and mixing sticks.

Give each staff member a coffee mug as a gift. After the break, start a Coffee Club where the staff members can continue to enjoy hot beverages. "The result is that staff are giving up going to Starbucks before work and are coming to school early . . . conversations are happening in the workroom again . . . teachers, custodians, and other staff are feeling incredibly spoiled." *(Sherry Billings, Odessa Middle School, Odessa, MO)*

Popcorn Treats

Throughout the year, serve the staff members popcorn and pickles in the lounge on Fridays. Often, you can borrow a popcorn popper from one of the school's parent organizations or purchase one for weekly use. "It smells heavenly, is a great treat, and gets us in the spirit for Friday football games." *(Virginia McDaniel, Goliad Independent School District, Goliad, TX)*

Another variation is to mix M&Ms chocolate candy in with the popped popcorn. The salty taste mixed with the sweet taste is wonderful!

Make Monday a Special Day

Make Monday a special day and not a *Moan*-day! Serve nice treats while you play Monday music such as "Monday, Monday" (by The Mamas and the Papas), "Rainy Days and Mondays" (by The Carpenters), "Manic Monday" (by The Bangles), "Come Monday" (by Jimmy Buffet), "I Don't Have to Be Me 'Til Monday" (by Steve Azar), or "Blue Monday" (by Fats Domino).

Muffin Monday

Meet staff members at the door on Monday morning with a smile, a friendly greeting, and a tray of muffins. Set the tone for a very good week. Don't do this every Monday because it will become expected, but do it periodically. You can substitute bagels and M&Ms for the muffins. (Does M&M stand for *Monday morning?*)

Milk Shake Mondays

On designated Mondays, invite the staff members to join together for *Milk Shake Monday.* Serve a variety of flavors of milk shakes. And remember to put the whipped cream and cherry on the top! Enjoy the sweet treats while socializing.

Monday Munchies

Divide the staff members into teams and have each one sign up for a Monday. On the selected Monday, have group members bring munchies to the staff lounge to share with their colleagues. These could include items such as a party mix, cookies, cupcakes, chips and dip, hot and cold appetizers, and so on. Each group could provide recipes for the items they prepared in order to compile them into a *Monday Munchies* cookbook.

Monday After Class

Start the week with a nice gathering on Monday afternoon, after the students have left. Have staff members take turns providing snacks, and simply catch up and get to know each other better. You might set some rules if you like, such as only positive topics may be discussed or no school topics may be brought up—it is just a social time.

For a Cause

Sleepy Hollow Elementary School coined the first Tuesday of each month as *Pink and Jeans Tuesday.* Principal Anastasia Epstein explained, "Wearing jeans is something that we typically save for Fridays (Spirit Days). However, staff may choose to wear pink and jeans on the first Tuesday of the month. If they choose to wear jeans, they contribute a dollar to the breast cancer support fund. At the end of the year, the money is sent to the Susan G. Komen Breast Cancer Foundation." *(Anastasia Epstein, Sleepy Hollow Elementary School, Sleepy Hollow, IL)*

PASSIONATE FOR PINK

Staff at Sleepy Hollow Elementary School, Sleepy Hollow, IL

Address the Stress

There is stress in all jobs, but there are times in the school year when the tension runs higher. Often, there isn't much that can be done to relieve the stress, but it can help to just acknowledge that it's there. Here are some ideas to acknowledge stress in the workplace.

Turn the Stress Around

In advance, make two sets of letters. Put each letter of the word *stressed* on large pieces of paper. Then put each letter of the word *desserts* on large pieces of paper. (Note: they are the same letters but in reverse order.)

Select eight staff members to take part in this activity with you. Pin the letters of the word *desserts* on the backs of the staff members. Then, have them hold the papers in front of them that spell out the word *stressed*. (Double-check that you have people in the correct order—front and back.)

Gather all staff members. Have your volunteers stand in the front of the room displaying the *stressed* sign. Talk about recent school events and tell the staff members how much their efforts are appreciated. Then tell them that you want to "turn the stress around."

Play Gloria Estefan's song "Turn the Beat Around." When it gets to the part where she sings "turn the beat around," have the group sing "turn the stress around." Have the eight people turn around and display the same letters in reverse order, spelling *desserts*.

> Praise is like sunshine to the human spirit: we cannot flower and grow without it.
>
> —*Jesse Lair*

Then serve desserts for everyone to enjoy—and have extras to take home.

Whine and Cheese Party

When you feel and hear a lot of grumbling at work, host a *whine* and cheese party. Serve cheese, fruit, crackers, and sparkling grape juice. But don't allow it to be a complaining session—just a stress reliever.

Stress Down Days

Tell staff members that the next day—or better yet, the rest of the week—will be Stress Down (casual dress) Days!

Staff Meeting Fun

Although attendance at most staff meetings is mandatory, enthusiasm is sometimes missing. Have you wondered what the formula for enthusiasm is? There are two important items that should be included to help people look forward to staff meetings:

1. Feed them—have food and beverages available.

2. Make it FUN! Include some time for attendees to enjoy each other's company, unwind, and change gears from the day's events.

"What is the meaning of poorly attended staff meetings?"

© Aaron Bacall

Five Minutes of Fun

Make a calendar of staff meetings. Ask volunteers to sign up for a meeting in which they will take responsibility for starting off the meeting with something fun. It could be a song, joke, story, reading, or an activity such as the one that follows. The activities need to be in good taste, though, so they won't offend.

Group Massage

Before you get into the business of the staff meeting, ask people to stand up and form a single-file line or circle. Tell them to place

their hands on the shoulders of the person in front of them and give them a nice shoulder and neck massage. First, have them pretend they're making a pizza and kneading the dough. Then, have them switch to making gentle karate chops on the person's back, and end with light "raindrops." After a few minutes, have the group members turn around and give a massage to the person who is now in front of them. Oh, it feels so good to have some of the tension released!

Getting to Know Each Other

Ask each person to bring in a picture of him- or herself as a baby or a young child. Make the pictures into large, wearable buttons. Also, ask staff members to share a fact about themselves as a child (e.g., I was born in Turkey, I learned to ride a horse at age 3, I am the third of 12 children). Attach the fact with the picture of the person. Give each person a button and fact, making sure that no one receives his or her own picture. Group members mingle around the room asking colleagues a question related to the fact, such as "Are you the person who broke his leg by falling off of a tractor?" or "Were you the child who was in love with Elvis Presley and had posters of him all over your room?" If the person answers "yes," he or she is given the pin to wear. When the pins have all been given to the appropriate wearers, ask the group members to be seated. Then let each person stand up and introduce him- or herself, giving the interesting childhood fact.

Appreciation Sound-Off

Start staff meetings with a time to *sound off* about the things that have gone well since the last meeting.

The Fourth Be With You

Have a celebration on the fourth day of every month or during the fourth week of every month at the staff meeting. Encourage staff members to report the successes they have experienced or observed during the month. You could use the *Star Wars* theme and characters to add to the fun.

Hurrays and Vents

You could also have a *Hurrays and Vents* time at the start of each meeting. Staff members are provided time to share personal or professional achievements, or those of others. They may also vent one frustration about anything at work or in their personal life. It is not a discussion; it is simply a release.

Upholding Our Vision

The shared vision of staff members is important and needs reinforcing. Shelton Park Elementary School, in Virginia Beach, Virginia, supports their vision using popcorn during staff meetings. A supply of 12 to 15 bags of popcorn is made available. The principal begins by presenting the first bag of popcorn to a staff member who has done something special for the school. For example, the principal may honor a teacher who is tutoring students after school, which aligns with the school's vision of being "responsive to students' learning needs."

From there, any staff member can honor a colleague. The celebrations conclude when all of the bags of popcorn have been distributed. (Sharing the popcorn with others is appreciated by all!) *(LouAnne Metzger, Shelton Park Elementary School, Virginia Beach, VA)*

Start With the Mission Statement

Schools adopt mission statements that identify the purpose of the school, such as learning, social responsibility, and so on. Put your mission statement to the tune of "Macarena." Have the staff members join together to recite, dance, or sing your mission statement at the start of each staff meeting.

End-of-the-Marking-Period Review

At a staff meeting at the end of the marking period, allow time for staff members to share how they dealt with difficult situations with parents or students. Have the staff members vote on who receives a prize for the worst experience. Not only will colleagues learn from the difficulties of others, they will also look at having successfully dealt with adversity as a potential prize-winning event.

FALL CELEBRATIONS

Birthdays

Happy Burger Day

Have a birthday celebration where the featured food served is hamburgers and cheeseburgers with all of the fixings. Make a giant burger for the special birthday person.

A Gift of Years

When a person has a decade-advancing birthday (30, 40, 50, or 60), celebrate the uniqueness of the decade. Do *not* give "over the hill" presents, dress in black, or wear black armbands. Instead, make meaningful celebrations out of these events.

Give the birthday person the appropriate number (30, 40, 50, or 60) of a single item, such as the following:

- Tulip or daffodil bulbs
- Packets of flower or vegetable seeds
- Golf balls
- Balloons
- Suckers
- Candy bars
- Bubble gum pieces
- Snack-size packs of potato chips, pretzels, or cookies
- Packets of bath salts
- The corresponding number of weeks of a subscription to a magazine

Or present one item for each decade, such as (for a person turning 40):

- 4 books
- 4 picture frames
- 4 10-dollar gift cards
- 4-layer cake

Another idea to celebrate a 40th birthday is to use *40 Winks* as the theme and give a basket full of sleep products such as bath salts, sleep shades for the eyes, melatonin, lavender sheet spray, and so on.

> Wrinkles should merely indicate where smiles have been.
>
> —*Mark Twain*

Decorate a Tree

Give each person a long piece of fabric. Ask him or her to decorate and write a birthday wish on each piece. Tie the fabric pieces together to make a knotted garland. Drape the garland around a small tree or the branches of a tree as a table decoration.

Phone Keypad Serenade

How are your keypad skills? I'm not fast enough to get through the whole song so that you can actually tell what tune is being played, but some people are. Chances are that you won't have to get very far before the person on the other end breaks out laughing. When a staff member has a birthday, call him or her and play this keyboard serenade.

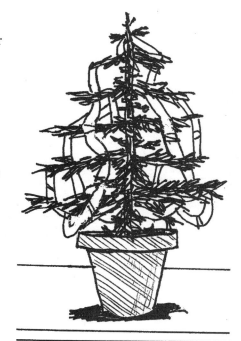

Happy Birthday to You!
1 1 2 1 6 3 1 1 2 1 9 6
1 1 # 9 6 3 2 # # 9 6 9 6

Don't try to leave a message with the keypad sounds—it just doesn't work.

By the Month

Gather the staff together in a large area that allows for movement around the room. Announce that when you blow the whistle, they are to get together with all of the other staff members who were born in the same month as they were.

When the members have found their groups, have them form small circles away from other groups. One at a time, call out each month and ask that group to give a cheer. (The reason you do this is to ensure that there is only one group for each sign and not two or more small groups that found each other.)

Each group is now responsible for planning a birthday celebration for the people who have a birthday in the month following theirs. For example, those who were born in January will plan a celebration for staff members who were born in February. Summer birthdays can be celebrated any time during the year—a surprise! Or for the summer birthdays, have an unbirthday party. The term *unbirthday* originally came from Lewis Carroll's *Through the Looking-Glass* and is associated

> Age is a number and mine is unlisted.
>
> *—Unknown*

with the song "A Very Merry Unbirthday to You" that was part of the Disney film *Alice in Wonderland.* An unbirthday is an event that is celebrated on a day that is not the person's birthday. So have an unbirthday party for summer birthdays.

Theme Birthdays

Plan celebrations that correspond to the recipients' passions. For example, if the person loves the beach, decorate with beach towels, make palm trees out of construction paper, and put up posters of beach scenes. Add some tropical music and punch with those cute little umbrellas. Have everyone dress in beach clothes (shorts, sandals, etc.).

Or perhaps the person loves baseball. Make the location into the "field of dreams" or a ballpark. Serve refreshments from a concession stand or have a couple of staff members act as vendors who yell "Hot dogs!" The perfect foods include hot dogs, popcorn, soda, nachos, and peanuts. To

add to the fun, you can have a pitching contest. Set up a pyramid of soda cans, draw a line to represent the pitcher's mound, and then have staff members try to knock over as many cans as possible with each pitch.

Or maybe the person collects figures of cows. Have a *moo-velous* celebration where everyone dresses in black and white. Serve Laughing Cow cheese on celery sticks as part of the refreshments. It is best not to bring in a real cow!

Announce It!

Local radio stations will often send out birthday wishes on the air. If they do this in your community, send a list of staff members' birthdays and ask that a greeting be sent over the airwaves.

Include happy birthday wishes in the morning announcements for the staff and students to hear.

Team Lunch

Give the birthday person and members of that person's instructional team an hour lunch to celebrate together.

Friday Cakes

Designate one Friday each month as the birthday celebration date. Have staff members take turns bringing in cakes for people who have birthdays during the month. One way to obtain volunteers is to have the staff members who had birthdays in a given month provide the cakes for the people who have birthdays the next month. For example, the people who have September birthdays provide the cakes for their colleagues who have birthdays in October.

Hide the Cards

Purchase a large supply of birthday cards and give one to each staff member. Ask them to write a birthday message wish and sign it. Collect the cards and, the night before or early on the morning of the birthday, hide the birthday cards everywhere around the person's work area—under the seat of a chair, behind or beneath a stack of books, in the file cabinet, under the computer—everywhere! The birthday person will have quite an exploration experience in locating the greetings.

Haywire Labor Day

Sometimes the best of plans go haywire. After a long weekend or holiday break, ask colleagues to share their traumas by completing the following sentence.

> My Labor Day weekend (or other weekend) was going great until _____.

Examples of holidays gone haywire include the following:

I received a call from my mother asking me to drive her to the hospital. She was coming out of church, looking in her purse for her sunglasses, missed the step, and broke her foot.

my son dislocated his shoulder playing football with his cousins.

I tried to light the grill and found that it was out of gas—and we had 20 people at our house for a barbeque.

the outdoor picnic was infested with a huge swarm of bees. Everyone had to move inside, and we don't have a house big enough for that many people.

School Lunch Week

Lunch Is on Us!

When your job is to make lunch for others every day, how nice it is to have it prepared for and served to *you!* During School Lunch Week in October, have the instructional staff members take up the kitchen and cafeteria duties so that the cafeteria staff members can enjoy a long (two hour) lunch away from school at a local restaurant. Include a note of appreciation with the invitation to have a *Lunch on Us! (Robert Graham, McHarg Elementary School, Radford, VA)*

Golden Utensils Award

Spray paint kitchen utensils with gold paint and present them to the food service staff members to acknowledge the amazing job they do!

Boss's Day

National Boss's Day is October 16th. When it falls on a weekend, it is usually celebrated on the working day closest to that date. It provides an opportunity for employees to recognize those in supervisory positions. Plan special events for those who hold supervisory positions.

King or Queen for a Day

Greet the boss in the parking lot with a red "carpet"—use red bulletin board paper as the carpet. Adorn the boss with a crown and take any items he or she is carrying into the building. Find out in advance what the person likes—beverages, snacks, desserts, and so on. Throughout the day, have these items delivered to the boss. Have a special lunch ordered in for the boss, and join him or her if possible.

You Are the Top Dog! or *You Are the Big Dog!*—Plan a lunch event in which you prepare hot dogs for the boss. Serve chili dogs for an added treat. *(Diane Nichols, Owen Valley High School, Owen Valley, IN)*

You Are the Big Cheese!—After the students leave for the day, have a celebration in which you serve cheese, crackers, and fruit. Give the boss either "cheesy" (funny) gifts or nice gifts that relate to cheese.

You Are the Top Banana!—Have everyone come to work wearing yellow clothes. Decorate a meeting room using bananas and yellow napkins and accessories. Serve banana splits or banana cream pies to celebrate the day.

You Are Our Kingpin!—The kingpin is the head pin of a triangular arrangement of bowling pins, or the chief person in a group. Have staff members wear bowling shirts and serve bar food such as nachos, popcorn, and so on. Wouldn't a bowling trophy be just the perfect gift for this occasion?

Sticky Note Celebration

Give each staff member a supply of brightly colored sticky notes. Ask each person to write down why he or she likes working with the boss. The notes could be titled "I like working with you because _____." The night before, or very early on the morning of Boss's Day, sneak in and decorate his or her office with all of the notes. In addition to placing them on furniture, pictures, and so on, put them in books and notebooks so that the notes will be found throughout the year.

You Go, Grill!

If your boss is female, have a grilling event. Cook hot dogs, hamburgers, bratwurst, and so on on a barbeque grill for all to enjoy.

Get-to-Know-Each-Other Holiday Celebrations

Often, schools open and the staff members don't know each other. This could occur when there is a consolidation of schools or when there's new construction. It is important to hold events where staff members continually become acquainted. This occurred at the

Alexander Hamilton Preparatory Academy, in Elizabeth, New Jersey, where the school underwent a complete change in staff. They decided that, to build camaraderie between staff members, they would celebrate each holiday by requesting that the people working on each floor of the building prepare the food for one designated holiday celebration. (Don't forget to include staff members who are not instructional staff, such as the security guards.) The staff members can choose to host a breakfast, lunch, snack, or their choice. "Food is the one common denominator that always brings people together." *(Janice Sutton, Alexander Hamilton Preparatory Academy, Elizabeth, NJ)*

End of the Marking Period

The end of each grading period is a marker event. Educators count them down as they progress through the year and reach their work-related goals. Celebrate these periods of success with special events.

A little note from me to you to thank you for all you do. The end of the grading period is almost here—a most perfect time to eat right and cheer!

Thinking of you,
Anastasia

Healthy Bodies = Healthy Minds

Provide staff members with motivational messages and both a healthy and a sweet treat to help them see that there is a light at the end of the tunnel! *(Anastasia Epstein, Sleepy Hollow Elementary School, Sleepy Hollow, IL)* To help you find just the right motivational quotes, refer to *Quote This!* (www.corwin.com).

Work Happy Hour

Plan a Work Happy Hour to celebrate the end of each marking period or semester. You can make up your own lyrics to well-known songs such as "I Heard It in the Break Room," sung to the tune of "I Heard It Through the Grapevine," and hold a group sing-along.

You can also form an employee band or choir and have them perform at the Work Happy Hour. Be sure refreshments are available for the entertainers and attendees to enjoy.

I Heard It in the Break Room
(sung to the tune of "I Heard It Through the Grapevine")

Oh, I'll bet you're wondering how I knew
'bout the change they're gonna put us through
This year will be different than before—all the things we did are out the door.
It took me by surprise I must say
That I have to teach a new way,
oh, yeah . . .

Chorus

I heard it in the break room
Where the atmosphere is gloom and doom
I don't want anyone to see
How worried this is making me
Worry, worry, yeah.
(I guess I really should embrace this)

I'll tell 'ya now I contend
With the new changes comin' in
Forget about the status quo—
The old ways have to go.
There are new issues facing us—fresh approach is a must
That's what . . .

Chorus

I hear in the break room
And it echoes through the restroom
I hope that everyone will see
How much fun change is gonna be
Yippee, Yippee, Yeah

Turn your cell phones and pagers off
We're about to have a lift-off
Be prepared to change and adapt
So put on your thinking cap
Don't be surprised when I say,
We're going to have to think a new way
'Cuz we . . .

Hear it in the break room
and the changes are coming soon
but the changes that we're going to see
will depend a lot on you and me . . .
mindset . . . mindset . . . YEAH!

Terry Doyle, Henderson, NV
and Patti Kenworthy, Stevensville, MI

Candy Corn Day

The day before Halloween, October 30th, is National Candy Corn Day, in celebration of the confection that was first produced in the 1880s by the Wunderlee Candy Company. More than 35 million pounds of candy corn is produced each year. Send a memo to staff members inviting them to attend a Candy Corn Day celebration. Have cups of the candy prepared for each person, as shown in the photo. In addition, give each teacher a bag of candy corn to share with his or her students. (*Anastasia Epstein, Sleepy Hollow Elementary School, Sleepy Hollow, IL*)

Halloween Spook-tacular Events

Ghostly Praise

Make ghost suckers out of suckers and facial tissue. Attach a note such as

"We don't stand a ghost of a chance of achievement without you!"

Fall Harvest Praise

Assemble packages of pumpkin candies and attach a note of appreciation such as

"Thank you for harvesting our students' potential!"

Secret Ghost

Two weeks before Halloween, send a notice to colleagues about the secret ghost activity you are planning. This notice will help you determine who is interested in participating. The following poem might accompany the notice. Change the days of the week in italic type as needed so that the final revealing takes place on Halloween. For example, in the poem shown, Halloween is on a Tuesday.

Halloween is almost here
So let's set out to spread some cheer.

On *Wednesday,* start with a card
Now surely, that won't be too hard.

On *Thursday,* brighten up the room
A decoration should lift the gloom.

On *Friday,* bring a little treat . . .
Something edible and fun to eat.

On *Monday,* there's a pumpkin theme . . .
Pretty simple, it would seem.

On *Tuesday,* bring a scary witch
To complete your task, without a glitch.

At half-past three we'll end the fun
By trying to guess the guilty one.
Can you pick the ghost that has been concealed?
On *Tuesday,* all will be revealed.

Once you know who will participate, have each participant write her or his name on a pumpkin-shaped piece of paper and place it into a plastic pumpkin container. Then, have each participant draw a name from the pumpkin; he or she becomes that person's Secret Ghost. During the week before Halloween, participants secretly give small items to the person whose name they drew, according to the plan described in the previous poem and the list below:

- Monday: a card
- Tuesday: a decoration
- Wednesday: something edible
- Thursday: a pumpkin-themed gift
- Friday: a witch-themed gift

The Secret Ghost might leave gifts in the recipient's mailbox, on his or her desk, or pinned to a classroom bulletin board. Or the Secret Ghost might have the gift delivered by another person.

At the end of the week, gather all participants so they can guess the identity of their Secret Ghost and see if their guesses are correct before they give the last gift of the week in person. *(Jeri Rohl, Decatur, MI)*

Variation 1

On the final day of the Secret Ghost activity, put all of the gifts together into a pile in the center of a circle. Have participants sit around the gifts and randomly select a gift to open and keep.

Variation 2

On the final day, have participants bring in canned goods to donate to a food bank for the community.

Ghostly Gifts

After staff members have gone home for the night, visit their classrooms or workstations. Hide a ghostly figure made out of construction paper or cheesecloth for them to find the next day.

Put the poem in a visible spot so they know to look for the ghost. When they have found the goblin, have them bring it to the office for a Halloween treat. *(Debra Macklin, Jennings Elementary School, Quincy, MI)*

Pumpkin-Growing Contest

You will need to plan for this activity long before autumn. Perhaps do the planting before the staff members leave for the summer and have volunteers water the pumpkin patch during that break. Prepare some land for planting and give each person a pumpkin seed or plant. Have each staff member plant his or her pumpkin and place a name marker in the ground to designate whose plant is growing there. Staff members may fertilize their plants, talk to them, give them love, play them music . . . whatever they think will make their plant grow. They may not, however, sabotage anyone else's plant. When Halloween arrives, give prizes for categories such as the biggest, best-shaped, smallest, or most uniquely shaped pumpkins.

While walking past the school last night
My eyes beheld a frightful sight.
On the wind floated a mournful sound
A shimmering mist swirled all around.
I think there may have been spooks in there
But enter and check? I did not dare!
So if you find your space is haunted
Capture the specter; be undaunted.
Bring it to the office—don't delay
And a sweet reward will come your way!

Pumpkin-Carving Exchange/Giving/Contest

Carving pumpkins can be a fun team activity to have in lieu of a staff meeting. The Web site www.extremepumpkins.com is a great resource for pumpkin-carving ideas such as the pumpkin hamburger shown in the cartoon.

Variation 1

Staff members can participate in a pumpkin exchange. Have staff members draw names to determine recipients. Have each person carve a pumpkin for the person whose

HAPPY HALLOWEEN
You probably haven't had time to carve a pumpkin,
and no Halloween is complete without one.
So here's a special one for you. I hope you enjoy it.
There is a flameless candle inside,
Turn out the light, and enjoy the sight.

name he or she selected. They can be personalized to match the person and his or her interests.

Variation 2

You can surprise someone with a carved pumpkin with a flameless candle inside and a note attached.

Variation 3

Host a staff pumpkin-carving contest between curricular areas or grade levels. Invite the superintendent to be the judge. *(Jackie Russell, Pleasanton Independent School District, Pleasanton, TX)*

Toasted Pumpkin Seeds Snack

What do you do with all the pumpkin seeds once you have carved the pumpkins? Toast them to make a delightful treat! Here's how:

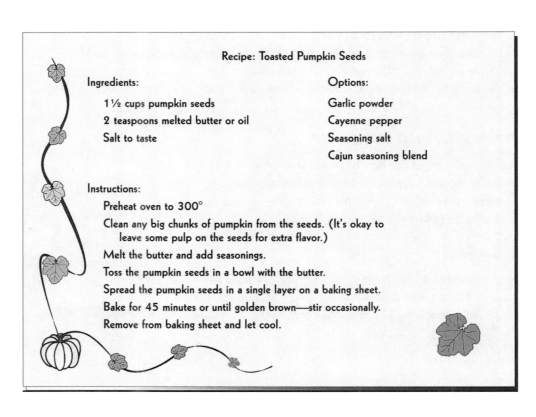

Recipe: Toasted Pumpkin Seeds

Ingredients:

1 ½ cups pumpkin seeds
2 teaspoons melted butter or oil
Salt to taste

Options:

Garlic powder
Cayenne pepper
Seasoning salt
Cajun seasoning blend

Instructions:

Preheat oven to 300°
Clean any big chunks of pumpkin from the seeds. (It's okay to leave some pulp on the seeds for extra flavor.)
Melt the butter and add seasonings.
Toss the pumpkin seeds in a bowl with the butter.
Spread the pumpkin seeds in a single layer on a baking sheet.
Bake for 45 minutes or until golden brown—stir occasionally.
Remove from baking sheet and let cool.

Theme Costumes

Staff members have fun dressing up for Halloween. This year, try having a staff costume theme. For example, the administrators could dress as doctors or nurses and all of the staff members could dress as patients. Or use the *101 Dalmatians* theme: the administrators dress as the parents and everyone else is a Dalmatian puppy. Or the administrators dress up as rock stars and the staff members dress up as fans.

You could also have a general theme such as the following:

- Wild, Wild West!
- Restaurant workers—cooks, servers, dishwashers, maître d'
- Circus animals
- Pirates
- Witches
- Famous people from history
- Music madness—a favorite musician, singer, instrument, and so on
- TV shows of the '50s, '60s, '70s, and '80s
- Decades—Select a specific decade and let teams choose anything that happened in that decade (e.g., music, books, music, food).
- Musicals
- Reality shows
- Children's books—Dr. Seuss, Harry Potter, and so on
- Countries—Teams select a country and dress in the attire associated with the country.
- Wild World of Sports—Divide the staff into teams so that each team represents a sport and dresses in that attire. For example, the football team could have refs, cheerleaders, players, fans, hotdog sellers in the stands, and so on. Golfers could wear green jackets, and auto racers could have pit crew members. Other sports that could be represented include basketball, soccer, hockey, tennis, horse racing, boxing, volleyball and beach volleyball, cycling, skiing, and track and field.

One principal in Alaska (who will remain unnamed) got into the Halloween costume theme each year. One year he came dressed as Batman—tights and all. The next year he dressed as Captain Jack Sparrow from the movie *Pirates of the Caribbean*. You might remember that, in the movie, actor Johnny Depp had dreadlocks and a braided beard. So . . . the principal superglued braids to his face. While he looked the part for Halloween, he sported two round bald patches on his face for several weeks after he had to pull the braids off on November 1st.

Who Is It?

Reinforce the push for literacy by having the staff members all dress up as favorite characters from a book or as a favorite author. When students guess the book or author correctly, they win prizes throughout the day. *(Jennifer Buteyn, Ridgewood High School, Norridge, IL)*

Ooey, Gooey, Scary Treats

Make an assortment of fun treats that are *ooey, gooey,* and *scary.* They can be gummy worm cupcakes, mud pies, ghost suckers, and so on. Decorate the table with wickedly creative pumpkins and gourds. You could have a school club sponsor this event or have the staff prepare the treats.

School Decorating Contest

Divide the staff into teams that will challenge each other for the best Halloween decorations. Let each team draw for an area of the school to decorate, such as the staff lounge, office, entry of the school, and so on. You can select a theme for the entire school or allow each area to have its own theme. Themes could be either specific to Halloween or general. Examples are *Haunted Luau, 1980s Prom, Spooky Hollywood* (red carpet style), *The Wizard of Oz* with many munchkins, *Private Eyes,* or *Home With the Addams Family.*

Pumpkin Patch

Make a pumpkin patch out of balloons in the main office. Put the name of a staff member on each pumpkin. Decorate the office with other items, such as witches and ghosts, and call the principal's office "Dracula's Den" or "The Dungeon."

Pumpkin Hunt

Cut out 30 patterns of pumpkins—10 each of three different colors of paper, such as orange, yellow, and green. Using markers, draw fun faces on each one. On the reverse side, do the following:

Write the number 1 on the back of the orange pumpkins.

Write the number 5 on the back of the yellow pumpkins.

Write the number 10 on the back of the green pumpkins.

Hide the pumpkins around the room before the staff members show up for a meeting. When they arrive, tell them to find as many of the pumpkins as they can before you say "Stop!" When they are done, have each person add up the numbers on the backs. The person with the highest number of points wins a prize.

You could also use real pumpkins and gourds and then let the staff members use them as room decorations.

Veterans Day

Veterans Day is usually observed on November 11th. Honor staff members who have served or are serving in the military by giving them a boutonnière or corsage with red, white, and blue ribbon. Ask staff members and students to wear red, white, and blue that day. When the students leave, invite all staff members to share a cake decorated as the American flag or serve red, white, and blue cupcakes.

Tie on an Apron Day—The Day Before Thanksgiving

Tie on an Apron Day is to celebrate the spirit of earlier generations of women who wore aprons as a symbol of home and family. Have the staff members who wish to participate draw names anonymously. The day before Thanksgiving, have each person wrap a loaf of bread in an apron, place a note of encouragement or praise in the pocket for the person whose name he or she drew, and anonymously deliver the package. Have all staff members wear their aprons on that day. For more information, go to www.apronmemories.com.

Thanksgiving

A long-awaited break is just around the corner. As it approaches, use one or more of these ideas to let colleagues know you are thankful for the opportunity to work with them, to focus on gratitude, to eat too much, and to have fun!

Words of Thanks

Make paper cutouts in the shape of turkey feathers. Write a personal note to each staff member that tells why you are thankful that he or she is on the staff. If these are comments that may be made public, each teacher might add his or her feather to a turkey body posted on the wall of the staff lounge.

Card of Thanks

Variation 1

Mail each staff member a Thanksgiving card. In it, write why you are thankful that he or she is on the staff. *(Jarcelynn Hart, Rosa Parks Elementary School, Woodbridge, VA)*

Take the time to identify the specific behaviors that each person does that you appreciate. Don't just write a generic "I appreciate you" or "You are appreciated!" Finish the sentence: "I appreciate you because _____." This will be a great self-esteem builder and will let that person know that you have noticed the good things he or she has been doing.

Variation 2

The week before Thanksgiving, mail *A Note From the Principal* to the spouses, significant others, parents, or children of each staff member. On the note, thank them for supporting their mom or dad, wife, husband, or partner as a staff member of the school. *(Don Ortman, Rock Valley Community School District, Rock Valley, IA)*

All-School Luncheon

Celebrate Thanksgiving and show appreciation for the staff and students by having a Thanksgiving luncheon. Students may bring in food items or donate money for meats that are cooked by school personnel. This makes the students feel that they're part of the celebration. When the meal is ready, everyone in the school eats

> Of all of the attitudes we can acquire, surely the attitude of gratitude is the most important, and by far the most life-changing.
>
> —*Zig Ziglar*

together. "Students love it and some say that this is the only time they will sit down with others for a Thanksgiving meal. It is a time to socialize with friends—a wonderful annual event." *(Janet Hodge, Academy for Technology and Academics, Conway, SC)*

Surprise Pies

Have an assortment of pies (pumpkin, squash, blueberry, apple, etc.) in the staff lounge for members to enjoy. You might even do this a week in advance of Thanksgiving and give each staff person the opportunity to order a pie for the holiday. Make the pies available on the day before the break.

Leftover Lunch

What to do with all those Thanksgiving leftovers? Plan a Leftover Lunch for the Monday after Thanksgiving.

Attitude of Gratitude

One of the best things you can do for yourself is to feel and express gratitude and appreciation. It helps to take time to reflect on what we already have; those positive thoughts lead to more positive events.

Give each staff member a sheet of paper titled "In my job, I am grateful for _____." (One gratitude surely will be that they have a job to go to.)

On the reverse side, title it, "In my life, I am grateful for _____."

Some things they might list include the following:

- A hot shower
- Laughing so hard it hurts
- Hearing a favorite song on the radio
- Lying in bed and hearing the rain hit the roof
- The Snow Day call
- Hot towels
- Reaching in your pocket and finding money
- Watching a baby sleep
- Swinging on swings
- The smell of fresh-baked bread
- Special e-mails from friends

Gratitude Journals

Introduce the idea of keeping a daily journal of things for which you are grateful. It doesn't have to be a long, diary-style journal. At the end of the day, simply complete the sentence: *The best thing about today was* _____. This allows staff members to reflect on the good that happens in their lives each and every day. Then, on the days when they feel unappreciated or it seems like nothing good is happening in their lives, they can pull out their journals and review the pervious month's entries. This simple act can change an attitude for the better.

> The more you praise and celebrate your life, the more there is in life to celebrate. Be thankful for what you have; you'll end up having more. If you concentrate on what you don't have, you will never, ever have enough.
>
> —Oprah Winfrey

Staff Journals

Place a journal in the staff lounge or in another location where staff members congregate. Encourage them to write an entry in the journal whenever they see something that makes them smile, warms their hearts, or makes them proud to work in education. This can de done during the week of Thanksgiving, and the results can be read at a staff meeting, or it can be an ongoing activity. At the end of the year, compile the entries and give a copy to each staff member.

I awoke this morning with devout thanksgiving for my friends, the old and the new.

—*Ralph Waldo Emerson*

CHAPTER 4

Wondrous Winter

December Through March

PAUSE FOR APPLAUSE

The Medium is the Message

Find small items at a discount store or in novelty catalogs, such as Oriental Trading Company (www.orientaltrading.com). Think of creative ways to express appreciation using the item you've selected. American and Canadian educators came up with many phrases to accompany items for staff members (see what follows). If you would rather just print out cards with artwork to accompany the items, you can order a CD of cards from www.thresholdgrp.com. These expressions of appreciation can be handed out at staff meetings, placed in classrooms or work areas for staff members to find when they arrive in the morning, put in mailboxes, attached to paychecks, and so on. They can be given to the staff as a whole or on an individual or team basis as the occasion arises.

Notepads/Notebook

We *note*-iced all your work this year. Thank you!

We are taking *note* of the great job you are doing!

You are a helpful reminder of why I love my job.

You *pad* the success of our school.

You did a *noteworthy* job.

Packet of Aspirin

Thank you for your hard work. I know it's been a headache.

You do more for my heart than taking aspirin. Thank you!

You are *aspiring*.

You take out the pain of _____.

Package of Batteries

Thanks for your enthusiasm. You really *energize* the whole staff.

Your *energy* keeps on going and going.

Your classroom was really *charged* today.

You really are an *ever-ready* teacher!

Your classroom was really charged today.

Snow Globe

I know you're really feeling *snowed* under. Can I help?

S'no secret what a great job you're doing!

There's *snowbody* like you!

You really *shake* things up!

Pushpins or Tacks

Great job! Thanks for the extra *push*.

Thanks for being so *tack-ful*.

Tape Measure

By every *measure*, you're great!

You more than *measure* up!

Few *measure* up to you!

You more than *measure* up!

Adhesive Bandages

Together we can heal any *boo-boos*.

I'm sorry. I may have hurt your feelings.

You are the best teacher's aid!

Here's to you for coming through that *scrape* on top.

Candle

You *light* up the lives of our students!

Small Mirror

This person is a very special teacher!

In my o-*pen*-ion, our staff is the BEST!

Pen

In my o-*pen*-ion, our staff is the best!

Thanks for helping write the futures of our students!

Diamond Decoration

You are a *real gem*.

Note: During the holidays, some discount stores carry plastic diamond decorations. Teachers love to collect the sizes. (*Tammy White, Grandfalls-Royalty Independent School District, Grandfalls, TX*)

Thank you for staying late to help me!

Paycheck Messages

All staff members receive a paycheck, so you can take advantage of this medium and make it a vehicle to express specific appreciation. Print messages on the check or enclose a sheet in the pay envelope that recognizes achievements such as good attendance. You can also send holiday messages or share educational jokes.

Call Home

Leave messages on staff members' answering machines at home. Express praise or a thank you. It will be nice for the staff member to come home to this message.

Pass the Vinegar

Fill a stylish or fancy bottle with vinegar. Each month, pass it from a staff member or group of staff members to another individual or group who overcame a *sour* (difficult) obstacle. The sour event is not identified, but the person(s) handing it off may say something funny that lets everyone know that this individual or group took a negative and made it into a positive. (*Cheryl Zigrang, Thoroughgood Elementary School, Virginia Beach, VA*)

The Secret Brush-Off

It's hard enough to just get through the winter with the cold, snow, ice, and sleet, but brushing off the snow and scraping the windshield at the end of a work day gets to be a laborious task. Select a day when it has snowed. Leave the building before the staff members and brush off their windshields. You might want to ask the custodian to help or have the recognition team do this activity with you. What a nice treat for the end of the day, and the staff will wonder who did it. (*John Speeter, Gentiva Health Services, Kalamazoo, MI*)

Smiling begets a warmer (work, home) environment.
Thanking begets an environment of mutual appreciation.
Enthusiasm begets enthusiasm.
Love begets love.
Energy begets energy.
Wow begets Wow.
Optimism begets optimism.
Honesty begets honesty.
Caring begets caring.
Listening begets engagement.

—Tom Peters

Pass the Praise

Create a duplicate set of cards with positive characteristics, such as *positive attitude, helpful, goes the extra mile,* and so on, written on them. Select an appropriate card to give to an individual who reflects that trait. You can either give it to the person privately or read it in front of a group. Give the individual both sets of the characteristic cards with the instructions to keep one card for him- or herself and give the duplicate card to another staff member. This helps to create a culture of praise and positive recognition. *(Jane Winter, Minglewood Elementary School, Clarksville, TN)*

Here is a starter list of positive traits you could use:

Creative

Dependable   Adaptable

Energetic   Resourceful

Optimistic   Punctual

Imaginative   Handles pressure well   Helpful

Self-confident

Willing to learn

Fun to work with

Versatile   **Friendly**

Risk taker   Flexible

Open-minded   **Patient**

Confident   Courteous

Good listener   **Sense of humor**

People oriented   Honest

Conscientious   Tactful

Efficient   Relates well with others

Trustworthy

Reliable

Able to get along with others

Versatile

Twinkie Toss

The lion is the mascot at Laurel Ridge Elementary School, in Fairfax, Virginia. Staff members are encouraged to submit *Roar of Approval* notes on which they cite positive actions that colleagues have done for each other, the community, the school, and so on. At each staff meeting, names are drawn from the container holding the Roar of Approval notes. Principal Larry Burke shared that "this part of the meeting has become known as the *Twinkie Toss*. . . . There are 10 Twinkies in a box so, one at a time, 10 names are drawn. With each one, the good work is shared with the staff and then a Twinkie is tossed to the recipient. Lots of fun. Very positive." (*Larry Burke, Laurel Ridge Elementary School, Fairfax, VA*)

Convention Attention

I love to speak at conventions because I believe everyone deserves to get away for a while and to be exposed to new learning. What is not always appreciated is what it takes to be able to get away. Lesson plans have to be prepared for subs, children's schedules have to be managed, carpools organized, family dinners prepared in advance, travel details arranged (and airport stresses overcome). Send a note to the hotel where staff members will be staying so that it is there when they arrive. Let them know you appreciate their effort and hope they have a good time learning.

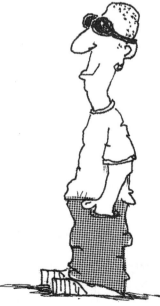

Bright Future Party

When the school's test scores are in or you have another event to celebrate, do it with a *Bright Future* theme. When the staff members come to the event, give each person an inexpensive pair of plastic sunglasses to wear. Attach a note that says, "Our students' futures are so bright, we have to wear shades," and have the song "The Future's So Bright, I Gotta Wear Shades," by Timbuk3, playing in the background to help set the tone and energize the staff. Have fun celebrating your success.

Theater Day

As an appreciation event, transform the cafeteria or media center into a theater with comfortable chairs. Design a simulated movie ticket with a note of appreciation on the back. Show a film and be sure to offer "movie food," such as popcorn, nachos, candy, and soda, to staff members while they enjoy the show. (*Elisa Pacheco, Truman Price Elementary School, Donna, TX*)

You may want to show movies that take place in a school setting, such as *Grease, Mr. Holland's Opus, Pay It Forward, Dead Poets Society, School of Rock*, and so on.

Reflection Folders

Provide all staff members with a purple folder to keep at their workstations. Ask them to place every card, letter, positive note or e-mail, article, and so on in their folders as they are received. As the year and their careers progress, staff members may experience frustrations and disappointments that can result in them not feeling good about themselves or their career choice. Encourage them to read the contents of their folders and reflect on those expressions of appreciation. (*Dana Ford, Madison Elementary School, Muscatine, IA*)

> One kind word can warm three winter months.
>
> —*Japanese proverb*

 ## POWERED BY FUN!

Welcome Back Breakfast

Host a Welcome Back Breakfast for staff members on the first day they return from the winter holiday. Serve quiche, bagels, fruit, and other goodies to start the new year. (*Mary Lou Cebula, Central School, Warren, NJ*)

The winter break was over and the teacher was asking the students about their vacations. She turned to Johnny and asked what he'd done.

"We visited my grandmother in Kalamazoo, Michigan," he replied.

"That sounds like an excellent vocabulary word," the teacher said. "Can you tell the class how you spell Kalamazoo?"

Johnny thought about it and said, "You know, come to think of it, we went to Ohio."

New Year's Resolutions

We often make resolutions for things we want to do in the new year. It's easier to achieve a goal when you have encouragement. Ask staff members to set a personal or professional goal they would like to achieve during a designated time period. Examples could include: *I want to . . . lose ten pounds, learn how to use a software program,* and *organize my files.* Create a bulletin board featuring the staff members who have made them. Post their picture and their resolution. You may also want to have staff members report on the progress they make in achieving their goals.

> May all your troubles last as long as your New Year's resolutions.
>
> —*Joey Adams*

Spring Break Countdown

> The only thing bad about a holiday is that it is followed by a non-holiday.
>
> —*Unknown*

It does seem like a long time until spring break. If you want to have some fun counting down the days, you can download a countdown clock onto your computer. You and your colleagues can find this at www.yahoowidgets.com by searching for "due." You can also use this to count down the number of days until a special event such as the end of the year, an important project, and so on.

If you want a low-tech countdown, cut construction paper into the number of rectangular pieces that is equal to the number of days your are counting. In large, bold print, write a number on each rectangle. Staple or glue the strips into chains with the numbers in reverse order. This activity may remind you of when you were a child and made paper chains to trim Christmas trees and decorate classrooms. Drape the chain in a very visible spot, such as by the mailboxes, staff lounge, or office. Each day, remove a link in the chain to reveal the number of days remaining until the special event or date.

Soup-er Bowl Celebration

Invite staff members to dress in the colors of the Super Bowl team they're rooting for. Have a staff event in which volunteer staff members prepare and share their favorite soups, salads, and snacks at a *Soup-er* Bowl celebration. You can have the fight songs playing in the background and your own version of cheerleaders.

You could also show NFL blooper videos during lunch and snack on popcorn, peanuts, and pretzels.

National Clean Off Your Desk Day

January 14th is National Clean Off Your Desk Day. This is a perfect time to do a little spring cleaning.

You can have a cleaning event where all staff members are asked to purge their files, dust, and so on. Make sure you have cleaning supplies and large trash containers available. At the end of the day, have a gathering with snacks and award prizes for winners of categories such as the following:

- Most Improved Desk
- Greatest Number of Pounds of Stuff Thrown Away
- Oldest Memo Found While Purging or Cleaning Out Files
- Person Who Found a File Containing a Certain Word or Phrase

Post the winners' names in a public place—and be sure to take pictures.

Variation

While you are cleaning, keep in mind that some of the items you won't use might be treasures to another person. Sometimes staff members have changed grade levels, are preparing for retirement, or have received donations from parents or other community members. Have each person bring items they are no longer using from their classrooms, and display these goodies on tables set up for this event. Staff members can then select items that will be useful in their classrooms. All leftover items can be either donated or disposed of. (*Debra Macklin, Jennings Elementary School, Quincy, MI*)

The Oscars

The Academy Awards, commonly known as the Oscars, are presented in February of each year by the Academy of Motion Picture Arts and Sciences. The awards date back to 1929 and recognize professionals in the film industry. The ceremony is held on a Sunday night, and awards are given in categories such as production, acting, music, sound, costume and makeup, and so on. Within each category are subcategories such as best actor and actress in a leading role, best picture, and best actor and actress in a supporting role. The winners receive an Oscar, an 8.5-pound gold-plated statuette.

Hold a Hollywood event to celebrate the Oscars. Have everyone wear something glitzy, such as rhinestone earrings or a feather boa. Have paparazzi (using disposable cameras) capture the moments as the attendees arrive on the red carpet. Serve punch in champagne glasses and star-shaped cookies. Decorate the room with twinkling lights and hang stars from the ceiling.

You could also have an out-of-school Oscar party. Write down words, phrases, or actions that the Oscar recipients might mention or engage in repeatedly such as the following:

- Mom/dad/stepmother/stepfather
- Wife/husband/partner

- Son/daughter
- Wow!
- My agent
- I didn't expect to be here tonight (or some variation of this)
- Makes a political statement
- Has notes written on a piece of paper or small card
- Tells a childhood story

Have each guest draw a card. More than one person can have the same card. Make a large batch of popcorn. Give each person an empty bowl. Each time an Oscar recipient mentions a word or phrase or engages in an action on the list, the people with the corresponding card receive a serving of popcorn. Although this is often done as a drinking game, Monday is a school day, so popcorn works better.

Anti-Oscar Event

If you are sick of all the Hollywood hype, extravagance, and attention on fashion that happens before, during, and after the Academy Awards, then hold an Anti-Oscar event instead. Send out an announcement of the event on recycled paper or cardboard. Have staff-member hosts wear their oldest clothes—the kind worn for painting or doing yard work. Make it a potluck or have everyone bring in a cheesy snack where Cheese Whiz has to be an ingredient.

Read the Memos—Turn in Your Reports

When there is a long article in your staff newsletter, include an incentive that will encourage staff members to read it all the way through. Toward the end of the article add text that says, "See me for a prize." When the staff members tell you they read the article and saw the note, give them an early release form, a piece of candy, and so on. (*Cheryl Zigrang, Thoroughgood Elementary School, Virginia Beach, VA*) You can soften up your request for the submission of monthly reports by including seasonal humor with the memo. (*Wendy Doremus, Hudson Public Schools, Hudson, MA*) Need some fun resources? *Laugh Lines for Educators* and *Grin and Share It!* are packed with humor that you can use (www.corwin.com).

Head Shed Day

Designate a day in which the staff members dress like the principal, superintendent, business manager, and so on—complete with a brief case, calculator, and coffee cup (if applicable).

Mystery Lottery Tickets

Some areas of the school just always need some attention. No one wants to clean out the refrigerator because no one really knows how long the food has been in there. Coffee spills are frequent, and who actually lifts the paper cutter to dust under that office workhorse? Purchase a few lottery tickets and put them in places where attention would be appreciated but is seldom received. It may take a long time for the lottery tickets to be found, but when one is discovered, it should be reported to the full staff so the person can be acknowledged for going above and beyond. You could also attach a little note that says, "Thanks for the help! We appreciate it a Lotto!"

Stress Kit

There are many times in a school year when you can feel tension. Each person needs to have a Stress Kit to use on those days. Put the names of all the staff members into a container. Have each person draw a name (making sure that no one draws his or her own name) and create a Stress Kit for that person. The kit could contain items such as a packet of aspirin, a wind-up desk toy, squeeze balls, a CD, tea bags, money for the vending machine, a candy bar, or an aromatherapy item.

You could do the name drawing at the end of the school year and ask staff members to assemble the Stress Kit over the summer. They can be creative in how they decorate the kit and in what items they choose to include. The kit can also be customized with the specific types of items the recipient likes (e.g., candy, music).

Give Winter the Boot!

Winter seems to drag on for a long time. Add some fun by *giving winter the boot*. Have staff members wear a pair of their favorite boots to work. They can be fashion boots, Army boots, Ugg Boots, fishing boots, ski boots, slipper-style boots, hiking boots, and so on. Have a celebration at the end of the day and serve hot chocolate and snacks.

FUNshine Celebration

By January, summer can seem like nothing but a faint memory, and the upcoming summer can seem forever away. When this is the case, organize your own *FUNshine* celebration. Create an indoor paradise with beach and ocean décor. Have shells, tropical travel posters, and play summer-themed songs such as "The Summer of '69," "All Summer Long," and "Summer Nights." Staff members can wear clothes such as shorts, Hawaiian shirts, and sandals. Serve lemonade with paper umbrellas, popsicles, and ice cream sundaes.

Maggie Hodges

Dog Days of Winter

Ask staff members to bring in pictures of their dogs. Post the pictures and a list of owners, but don't identify the owner of each dog. Create ballots and have staff members submit their guesses as to who is the owner of each dog. You could expand this to be a schoolwide event, asking the students to vote as well.

You could also have a contest in which staff members vote in categories such as the following:

- Dog Juan (Most handsome)
- Diva Doggie (Prettiest)

- Dog that looks most like its owner
- Cutest outfit

Give the winners dog treats as prizes.

Teachers' Pets

Ask staff members to bring in pictures of their pets and make a bulletin board of them. List the name of the animal and the owner. Give participants pet treats to take home to their animals.

Remote Control Car Derby

Is it too cold to go out but you still want to do something playful? Have staff members who own (or whose children own) remote control cars compete in a race. Set up a course in the gym or cafeteria and see who has the fastest vehicle. Give prizes to the winners. Even if you don't race, watching the event will be great fun.

Bad Hair Day

We all have bad hair days—days when our hair seems to have a mind of its own or when we are rushed and don't quite style it the way we are supposed to. Give staff members a day when they don't have to worry about what their hair is doing. On this day, they can wear hats, scarves, wigs, or pigtails—anything that covers or compensates for their bad hair. Be sure to take pictures!

Monday Haircuts

You could follow up the bad hair event by having *Haircut Mondays*. Most salons are closed on Mondays, so ask to have volunteer stylists come to the school to give complimentary haircuts to staff members. *(Elizabeth Garza, Weslaco Independent School District, Weslaco, TX)*

End-of-the-Term Relays

Organize an end-of-the-term relay in which staff members compete in tasks such as alphabetizing a list of names, matching comments to report cards, averaging grades by hand, and solving a riddle. *(Elisabeth C. Thompson, Callaghan Elementary School, Covington, VA)*

100th Day of School

The 100th day of school usually falls in mid-February. It varies by district depending on when classes begin. There are many activities provided on the Internet for teachers to incorporate the use of 100 in their lessons. On this day, have staff members (and students) dress up like they would if they were 100 years old. Arrive at school with a walker, cane, glasses, handbag, shawl, bow tie, costume jewelry, knee-high nylons with a dress, slippers, handkerchief, and so on.

Variation

Make a book of the *100 Things I Like About Working at _____ School*. Have staff members submit entries of what they like most about working at the school. Compile the best 100 into a booklet to give to staff or make a bulletin board from the responses.

Chocolate Fairy

Yum, Chocolate!

Designate a person(s) to serve as the Chocolate Fairy. Throughout the year, have the Chocolate Fairy leave surprise chocolates for staff members in places such as the mailboxes, classrooms, workstations, lounge, or in pay envelopes. Have the fairy attach a note indicating that the treat is from the Chocolate Fairy. It makes for a wonderful afternoon or end-of-the-week "pick me up." *(Teresa Stump, Sunnyside Elementary School, McKenney, VA)*

Pantry Potluck

Have staff members sign up to participate in a series of potlucks. Divide the members into groups of five or six, depending on if they are serving a meal or a snack during the staff meeting. Have each staff member bring an item from his or her home pantry and either place it in a bag or wrap it. Assemble all of the items in one place and have each person select a package. The food item inside must be used in the dish individuals prepare for the potluck. For example, if a can of kidney beans is drawn, it can be used to make chili or a three-bean salad. If a jar of peanut butter is in the package, it can be used to make peanut butter and jelly sandwiches or peanut butter cookies.

The teams will need to meet and identify their ingredients to see if there is any theme they can create or if it is going to be a random potluck. Some strange food assortments might result, but it will be fun.

Alphabet Potluck

Have staff members sign up to participate in a series of potlucks. Divide the members into teams of five or six, depending on if they are serving a meal or a snack at the staff meeting. Have each team draw letters of the alphabet from a hat. On the day of the potluck, have each team bring in food that begins with those letters. This will make for some very interesting menus!

Progressive Dinner

On an evening when staff members have to work, hold a *progressive dinner.* Ask staff members to volunteer to prepare food and host colleagues in their classrooms. For example, the staff members have appetizers in one room, then move to another for soup, and then to another area for the main course. If you have a large staff, divide them into smaller groups and have several progressive dinners at the same time. (*Darlene Roll, Ohio Hi-Point Career Center, Bellefontaine, OH*)

> Having a good time is the best motivator there is. When people feel good about a company, they produce more.
>
> —*Dave Longaberger*

Out to Lunch

Once a month, select staff members to go out for a 90-minute lunch. A different group is selected each week; the groups change every month. Have the remaining educators cover the classrooms for those who are out to lunch. This is an excellent way for staff members to get to know each other better—and to relax. (*Sandra Hensley, Tenderfoot Primary School, Sanger, TX*)

Sweet Payday

When the paychecks are placed in the envelopes, surprise the staff members by including a wrapped piece of candy. Life Savers candies work well, and the message is nice.

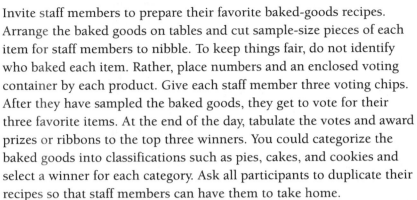

Staff Member Bake-off

Invite staff members to prepare their favorite baked-goods recipes. Arrange the baked goods on tables and cut sample-size pieces of each item for staff members to nibble. To keep things fair, do not identify who baked each item. Rather, place numbers and an enclosed voting container by each product. Give each staff member three voting chips. After they have sampled the baked goods, they get to vote for their three favorite items. At the end of the day, tabulate the votes and award prizes or ribbons to the top three winners. You could categorize the baked goods into classifications such as pies, cakes, and cookies and select a winner for each category. Ask all participants to duplicate their recipes so that staff members can have them to take home.

This activity works well on parent-teacher or inservice days when the students are not in attendance and there are opportunities to taste the products throughout the day. You could also change this to be a breakfast casserole cook-off or other item to have during nonstudent days.

Taco Tuesday

Prepare the meat portion of tacos, and have staff members sign up to bring in the remaining ingredients—tortilla shells, shredded cheese, chopped onions, chopped tomatoes, sour cream, taco sauce, salsa—for a Taco Tuesday.

Popcorn Surprise

Give staff members gift bags that contain popcorn. Attach a note to the bag that says, "Remember to feed your mind." (*Sherry Billings, Odessa Middle School, Odessa, MO*)

Sick Day

Have a *Sick Day* on which you provide staff members with hot chicken soup, vegetable soup, bread, and ginger ale for lunch. This will cure what "ales" everyone during the winter.

Marumsco Hills Elementary School, in Woodbridge, Virginia, added to this fun event by purchasing giant microbes: stuffed animals that look like tiny microbes—only a million times the size—available from www.schoolnursesupplyinc .com. Each staff person received their own stuffed version of The Common Cold, The Swine

Flu, The Flu, Sore Throat, Stomach Ache, Cough, Ear Ache, Bad Breath, Athlete's Foot, and so on. *(Joanne Alvey, Marumsco Elementary School, Woodbridge, VA)*

New Year's Resolution Teams

At a group event such as a staff meeting, have each person complete a goal sheet. Explain that the goal they write down will be shared with at least one other person, so they shouldn't write deep secrets. The paper size should be at least 8 1/2 × 11.

Have people make paper airplanes out of their goal sheets. In case someone doesn't know how to fold paper into an airplane, provide a diagram. It could be put on a transparency for the group to see or copied on the reverse side of the goal sheet.

When the airplanes have been assembled, have the staff members fly their planes across the room. Each person retrieves an airplane and becomes the support person to assist the owner of the airplane in reaching his or her goal.

Follow-up: If you set a timeline such as one month or six months, have the teams report to the whole group at the end of the time period. Describe what the goal was and how it was achieved (e.g., Maggie wanted to lose ten pounds, and we are happy to report that she exceeded her goal and has lost twenty-two pounds through diet and walking two miles a day). You could also give status reports along the way on progress that's being made toward reaching the goal.

Financial Planning   Balance My Check Book   Exercise

Eat Healthier

Take a Vacation

My Goal:
(This will be shared with other people.)

Name: _____

Phone: _____ E-mail: _____

Department or grade level: _____

The goal I have set for myself is: _____

_____

_____

My time line is: _____

You can help me reach my goal by: _____

_____

Date Nights

Time for Friends

Run a Marathon   Lose Weight   Learn Excel

Meetings and More Meetings

Do you wake up in the middle of the night dreaming of yet another meeting you have to attend?

meeting... need meeting

must... meet   need... meet

By this time of the year, there have been many meetings, and there are many more ahead. Have a sing-along about meetings at a meeting. This song is sung to the tune of "Funiculi Funicula." You may not recognize the name of this song, but as soon as you hear the tune you will know it.

The Meeting Song
Sung to the tune of "Funiculi Funicula"

Some think . . . that we should never have a meeting.

Perhaps they're right; perhaps they're right.

The days . . . are awf'lly long, at times defeating.

My neck is tight; my neck is tight.

And now . . . we have to listen to announcements.

My mind is gone; my mind is gone.

Don't want . . . to hear important new pronouncements.

I need to yawn; I need to yawn.

Teaching, teaching, teaching can be tough,

Trying to explain a lot of stuff.

It can be tough; some days are rough; there's so much stuff; I've had enough.

Meetings in the afternoon are definitely tough.

Some say . . . that meetings aren't that necessary.

Perhaps it's true; perhaps it's true.

We sit . . . in one position stationary,

'Til we turn blue; 'til we turn blue.

We try to stay awake for every detail,

but it's a chore; but it's a chore.

And even though we catch up on our e-mail,

Our butts are sore; our butts are sore.

Prove it; prove it; prove it can be done.

Show me; show me meetings can be fun.

The day is done; it weighed a ton; it wasn't fun; I want to run.

Teaching can be tough; the day is done; we need some fun.

© Eric Baylin

Silly Putty Play Day

Place Silly Putty on the tables or desks when staff members arrive at a meeting. Don't say anything . . . just let them play. This is a fun premeeting stress reliever.

Balloon Animals

Invite a clown or someone who knows how to make balloon animals to school. Ask him or her to briefly teach staff members how to make a simple animal. How fun is that?!

New Names Tags

Give staff members name tags. Instead of writing their name, have them write the city they were born in and their pet's name. If they don't currently have a pet, they can use a previous pet's name or the name of a friend's pet. For example, my name tag would read *Wiesbaden Maggie.* Allow the staff members time to mingle while they enjoy some refreshments.

At another staff meeting, ask attendees to write just their middle name on the name tag.

Stress and Strainer

When the stress of the year gets you down, have a *Stress and Strainer* event. Give each person a strainer (colander), which they are to decorate any way they want. Plan a staff gathering with food and music. In order to be admitted, each person must wear his or her strainer.

Backwards Day

You will know when to call this day—it will be during a week when nothing seems to go right. Send a meeting notice to staff members with the message written backward.

Center Media the in 3:00 at Today Meeting Staff

This will not be an event that staff members will have prepared for, but ask them to wear something backward (e.g., a hat, name tag with their name written backwards, belt, or T-shirt). When they arrive at the meeting, acknowledge that it has been a crazy week and serve upside-down cake.

Find the Fun in Fitness

Most Weight Loss

The new year often brings a new or renewed commitment to fitness. Have staff members who volunteer for this activity because they want to lose pounds weigh in on the same day. Make a chart for each person to record his or her progress—all records are maintained on the honor system.

Each week, staff members contribute one dollar to the weight-loss fund and record their gain or loss for the week. If there is a weight gain, an additional dollar is put into the fund for each pound or a quarter is added for each quarter-pound gained. On the Friday before Spring Break, the person who has lost the most weight gets the money in the fund. (*Debra Macklin, Jennings Elementary School, Quincy, MI*)

> I signed up for an exercise class and was told to wear loose-fitting clothing. If I had any loose-fitting clothing, I wouldn't have signed up in the first place!
>
> —*Unknown*

100 Pounds Lighter

Divide staff members who are interested in participating into teams. Each team contributes a monetary amount, such as 10 dollars, and has the same goal—to lose an accumulative 100 pounds. Post a chart in the staff lounge so that each team can record its progress every week. The first team to reach the goal of losing 100 pounds receives the money collected.

If you want to implement a program that has already been developed, try the Dump Your Plump program (www .dumpyourplump.com).

To help in this process, form running or walking groups, schedule volleyball tournaments, organize basketball games, and so on.

Salad Bar Potluck

To help people achieve their fitness goals, have salad bar potluck lunches. Provide a sign-up sheet so that everyone knows what food items have already been spoken for. You can also ask a team to do the shopping together—this avoids having the type of miscommunication that results in an all-lettuce lunch.

WINTER CELEBRATIONS

Gifts of Time

Sometimes it feels like there just aren't enough hours in the day! Staff members often lament about not being able to get everything done—or even having time to catch a breath.

During my presentations, I conduct an informal survey of rewards the audience would like to receive. The *gift of time* is the top-ranked reward—in every state and in every type of audience. More than anything else, staff members value time with their families and flexibility in their schedules. Discretionary time at work is also valued; student-free and rest or relaxation times are also necessary. If you are looking for the perfect gift to give to your overscheduled staff members, consider giving the gift of time.

Half-Day Shopping Pass

To celebrate the holiday season, hold a drawing in which two half-day shopping passes are awarded during the November staff meeting. The certificates have a 30-day expiration date. Repeat the drawing at the December staff meeting as well. An even more special gift is having the principal cover the classrooms while the teachers are out shopping. *(Anita Brown, Stonington Elementary School, Stonington, IL)*

30-Minute Break Coupons

Give staff members a coupon for a 30-minute break. Have the principal, itinerant staff, or counselor read to the students during that half hour; this provides a short break for teachers and gives the students a different presence in the classroom.

Staff Gift Exchange

Have a yearly gift exchange with a different theme designated each time. Themes you might consider include:

- Crazy coffee mugs
- Holiday hats
- Calendars
- Holiday music CDs
- Holiday ornaments or decorations that correspond to the person's interests (e.g., computers, sports, reading)
- Musical items
- T-shirts
- Books

White Elephant Gift Exchange

Have everyone bring in a wrapped white elephant gift, and host the gathering.

Where did the term *white elephant* originate? According to Wikipedia (http://en.wikipedia.org/wiki/White_elephant), it came from the sacred white elephants kept by Southeast Asian monarchs. To have a white elephant was regarded as a symbol that the monarch was ruling with justice and that there was peace and prosperity. The animals were considered to be sacred and there were laws prohibiting their use for labor. So receiving a white elephant as a gift from a monarch was a mixed blessing. The animal was a symbol of being in the monarch's graces, but because the animal couldn't be used for labor, the receiver incurred a huge expense to maintain it.

Today, a white elephant gift is typically something lying around the house that you don't want or is a gag gift of some kind.

Put all the gifts in the center of a circle and allow everyone to choose a gift. Read the poem *The Night Before Christmas* aloud. Each time the word *the* is read, pass the gift you are holding to the right. Each time the name of a body part (e.g., nose, cheeks) is read, pass the gift being held to the left. At the end of the poem, staff members open the gift in their hands. There are "tremendous laughs both during the passing and the opening," reports Violet Tantillo. (*Violet Tantillo, Jefferson Elementary School, Berwyn, IL*)

Regifting

After returning from Winter Break, ask staff members to rewrap a gift they received during the holidays. Determine in advance whether the gifts are to be useful gifts or gag gifts. The gift exchange can be implemented in different ways.

Variation 1

Number each gift. Have each staff member draw a number and select the corresponding gift.

Variation 2

Staff members draw numbers. The person with "1" is the first to select a present from the stack. The person who draws "2" is next, and so on.

Letter to the Parents

Write a letter to the parents of each staff member that tells them about the positive things their child does for the school. Put the letter in a holiday card and mail it the week before Winter Break. "It was amazing the number of notes, cards, and phone calls I received. It did make a difference," says Janet Word. (*Janet Word, Childress Elementary School, Childress, TX*)

Jingle Their Bells

Give each staff member a holiday necklace: a jingle bell strung on yarn. Also give them a card on which they can write expressions of praise and appreciation. Have staff members write a message to one colleague and give him or her the note and jingle bell. If staff members receive multiple jingle bell necklaces, they can combine the jingle bells onto one strand of yarn or wear multiple necklaces. Staff members wear their jingle bells for the week before the Winter Break.

Variation

Another variation of this is to use this activity as a school or recognition committee FUNdraiser. In this scenario, students and staff members buy the jingle bell necklaces for 50 cents. When purchased, the students identify whom the necklace has been purchased for and write a note of praise and thanks to that staff member—the students do not actually receive the necklaces. Be sure to review the notes before they are delivered to sort out any pranks. Combine the jingle bells onto one or more strands of yarn and deliver them to the staff members or put them in their mailboxes. Staff members are asked to wear their bells for a week. "This can get pretty humorous!" notes Anglia Webb-Crosby, whose Future Educators implemented the activity with the staff. (*Anglia Webb-Crosby, Lowndes High School, Valdosta, GA*)

Shop and Lunch

Arrange for businesses and vendors to display their products during lunch times so that staff members can shop without leaving school. This is especially appreciated when held in December.

Gadget Day

Make arrangements for stores to set up displays of the gadgets available in their stores. Invite staff members to bring in their favorite gadgets to share with colleagues. This will help spark ideas for holiday shopping.

Sponsor a Family

Contact school counselors or social workers, local assistance agencies, or places of worship for a list of families who need help during the holidays. Make a list of the demographics of each family and have the school sponsor them. (Remember to also ask about pets—they're part of the family, too!) If you have pictures of the family, include them as well.

Post the list in the lounge so that staff members can sign up to bring in a gift for a designated person. Make sure that all family members receive gifts—not just the children.

Dress a Child

Make a holiday tree display with paper ornaments as decorations, and write the name of a clothing item, size, gender, and the age of the recipient (e.g., sweater, child size 10, girl, age 10) on each ornament. Have staff members select a clothing item(s) they would like to contribute. More expensive items such as jeans, jackets, and shoes could be jointly purchased by several staff members.

On the designated day, have staff members place the paper ornament on the unwrapped clothing item, and put them in a secure location, such as under a holiday tree in the staff lounge. At the end of the day, move the items to a place where they can be gift wrapped.

Twin Gift-Wrapping Contest

Wrapping the gifts to be delivered can be great fun. Set up tables as workstations for pairs of people. At each station, place gift wrap, a roll of tape, scissors, ribbon, and the gift to be wrapped. To make it fair, have the gifts to be wrapped placed in the same size box (such as a shirt box). Divide the staff members into pairs and have them stand at the tables. The two people are to stand next to each other with one arm around the other person throughout the wrapping process. Say, "Go!" The partners are to wrap their box with one person using only his or her right hand and the other person using only his or her left hand. The other hand has to remain wrapped around the other partner's waist. The winner is the first pair to completely wrap the present.

The 16 Days Before Winter Break

Put the names of each staff member into a basket 16 days before they leave for Winter Break. Draw a name each day and reveal that day's prize winner during the morning announcements. Prizes could include:

- Free coffee coupons
- Books
- Fun notebooks
- Candles
- Gift baskets
- Markers
- Poinsettias (*Sylvia Henderson, Ross Elementary School, Milford, DE*)

Holiday Sweater Day

Designate one day in which all staff members wear a holiday sweater to school. Let the staff members vote and give out prizes for the cheesiest sweaters.

Staff Scavenger Hunt

Prior to Winter Break, have a scavenger hunt for miniature or cutout Christmas trees and snowmen. Give the staff a few minutes to find as many of each as they can. Award the winners with tree and snowmen prizes. "It was really nice to see the smiles on their faces after a stressful start to the school year. It was a lot of fun!" added Principal Sylvia Henderson. (*Sylvia Henderson, Ross Elementary School, Milford, DE*)

A Cup of Christmas Tea Party

A Cup of Christmas Tea is a delightful book by Tom Hegg. It is written in a rhyming verse and tells the story of a man who reluctantly goes to visit his ailing great aunt. This time of year is so hectic, and he really doesn't want to go. But once he's there, he is surrounded by peace, love, and the joy of the season as the two distant family members share a cup of tea.

Place a tea cup in each staff member's mailbox and invite them to a tea party. Have them bring their tea cups to the gathering. Set the tables with finger sandwiches, teas, honey, sugar, cream, and so on. Read the book to the staff and then celebrate the season with a cup of tea and the other refreshments.

Talent Show Challenge

Many schools collect canned goods for local food banks during holiday times. At the St. Paul School, in Cana, Virginia, students added a new element. A goal was set for the number of cans that the student body was to collect. If they achieved that goal, then the administrators had to perform in a talent show. How fun would that be?! *(Nancy Wilmoth, St. Paul School, Cana, VA)*

Caption It!

Collect cartoons or pictures that relate to the holidays, such as the ones shown.

Remove any captions and text that may go with the pictures. Send the cartoons to the staff and ask them to write captions for the pictures.

Post each picture or cartoon on big sheets of shelf paper with plenty

of extra room for writing. Have a supply of markers handy so staff members can write in their captions. You can either have staff members identify their captions or have them be anonymous. You could make a contest out of it and have staff members vote for the best captions.

Build a School

Divide the staff into teams. Give teams the challenge of building gingerbread schools. There are a number of recipes and instructions for gingerbread houses on the Internet, but instead of designing a house, they will design schools. Give each team the same number of days to complete the task. Display the final products. You can

have them judged by an independent party, such as the superintendant, or have the students vote for their favorite.

Give the winners holiday-related gifts or treats (not made of gingerbread!).

Secret Santa

This annual event is always fun! Have participating staff members draw names and follow the guidelines for gifts to be given each day. You might want to put a price limit on the gifts: for example, a maximum of 3 dollars per day for Monday through Thursday and 10 dollars for Friday. (This "ceiling" prevents staff members from getting carried away with their purchases and, as a result, possibly making the group uncomfortable.) Setting limits also equalizes the purchases. Each day, the participants secretly deliver their gifts to the staff member whose name they drew. At the end of the week, everyone gets together to exchange the final gift. Each person guesses who his or her Secret Santa is and shares the clues discovered during the week.

Holiday Memo

To: All staff members

Date: Late November (after Thanksgiving)

Re: Secret Santa

It's that time of the year again! We need to start planning for Secret Santa week. The scheduled date for this event is the week of _____. For those of you who are not familiar with the Secret Santa activities, the following is a brief description of what it involves:

1. First, we draw names (only those who want to participate are included).

2. Beginning Monday, December _____, you discreetly give one gift each day to the coworker whose name you drew. (Monday through Thursday will have a theme that suggests the type of gift to give.) Gifts should range in price from 50 cents to 3 dollars per day.

3. On Friday, you bring a gift (maximum price of 10 dollars) for your person, and we will meet as a group (potluck lunch) and guess who our Secret Santa was.

Themes for Secret Santa Week

Monday—Decoration Day

Tuesday—Naughty or Nice

Wednesday—Goodie Day

Thursday—Musical Day

Friday—Meet Your Secret Santa

Continue the memo with information about how to be included in the Secret Santa event and when the drawing of names will be held. Guidelines for each day of the Secret Santa event can also be distributed in poem form as shown.

Secret Santa

Monday—Decoration

'Tis the season to be jolly,

Adorn with mistletoe and holly.

A gift to decorate a tree?

Nay, just one to decorate thee.

Tuesday—Naughty or Nice

Day one is over, the second is here,

Continue on with the season's good cheer.

This day's theme is *Naughty or Nice*.

Which shall it be? I needn't think twice.

Wednesday—Goodies

Candy and cookies, baked goods galore,

Any way possible we could want more?

Days so filled with yummies and sweets,

Let us partake of holiday treats.

Thursday—Music

Music, the gift by no means the least,

Brings joy amidst our merriment and feast.

Listen to the melodies of this season

Praising the holiday's reason.

Friday—General

Gifts we give to those so dear,

Friends and loved ones far and near.

To give others a holiday lift,

We select for them a small Christmas gift. *(Bill Warren, South Haven, MI)*

Variation

The variation of the Secret Santa event that I like the best is to give the person a toy on the final day. The toy is personalized to reflect the person's interests (e.g., animals, cooking). These toys are then donated to organizations such as Toys for Tots or the Salvation Army.

Noon Year's Eve

Schools are always on break around New Year's Eve, but often staff members plan get-togethers during that time. Are you someone who can't stay up until midnight to ring in the New Year? If so, plan a *Noon* Year's Eve celebration. Arrange a lunchtime event where staff members can get together to celebrate and share their resolutions for the new year.

A New Year's resolution is something that goes in one year and out the other.

—*Unknown*

Calendar Celebrations

Chase's Calendar of Events Annual is published every year. This day-by-day directory of special days, weeks, and months can be consulted to help you plan your own celebrations. Since there are so many designated celebrations, you might make a list and ask staff members to vote for the ones they are most interested in. Here are some of the many events you could celebrate in January and February:

January

- National Soup Month
- National Hobby Month
- National Book Month
- Hot Tea Month
- Oatmeal Month
- National Pizza Week (second week in January)
- National Bowling Week (second week in January)
- National Fresh Squeezed Juice Day (third week in January)
- Clashing Clothes Day
- Hat Day
- Secret Pal Day
- National Popcorn Day (January 31)

February

- National Cherry Month
- National Grapefruit Month
- National Snack Food Month
- Canned Food Month
- Carrot Cake Day (February 5)
- Pizza Pie Day (February 9)
- Random Acts of Kindness Day (February 17)
- Love Your Pet Day (February 21)
- Banana Bread Day (February 23)
- National Tortilla Chip Day (February 24)

Chinese New Year

Chinese New Year celebrations begin on the first day of the first month of the Chinese calendar. This is the day of the second full moon after the Winter Solstice. The 15-day celebration includes fireworks, firecrackers, food, candy, and gift-giving.

Create your own festival by sending staff members invitations decorated with pictures of dragons, firecrackers, Chinese images, and calligraphy. In your message, include the fact that in the Chinese tradition red clothes are worn to scare away bad fortune.

Transform your meeting area into a Chinese festival venue. Many traditional activities are associated with this holiday; make posters describing the traditions and display the Chinese calendar. Red and gold are symbols of luck and prosperity, so use them as your color scheme. Place red and black balloons around the room with gold ties.

Because it is a tradition to start the new year with a clean slate, make sure brooms and dustpans are out of sight to prevent good fortune from being swept away.

Set up a buffet with an assortment of Chinese foods. At one end of the table, place red plates and chopsticks wrapped with red napkins. At the other end, have beverages (including green tea) available in red cups. When planning the menu, keep traditional dishes with ingredients that have important meanings in mind. Make and display a sign to share these associations.

Dumplings represent wealth

Lettuce represents prosperity

Noodles represent longevity

Oysters represent receptivity to good fortune

Seaweed represents good luck

Whole fish represent abundance and togetherness

Tangerines represent good luck

Oranges represent abundance and togetherness

A new year is unfolding—like the blossom with petals curling tightly concealing the beauty within.

—*Edith Lovejoy Pierce*

"Trays of Togetherness" are also part of the celebrations. Families keep a tray of dried fruits and candies to share with visiting friends and relatives. Make a tray of fruit and goodies to share as well.

And remember the fortune cookies! If you have enough time before the celebration, you can order fortune cookies with specialized messages.

Flowers also play an important role in the celebrations. Peonies symbolize love, affection, and beauty. Use silk flowers to adorn the buffet table or put them in vases on the dining tables. (One traditional belief is that if a peach blossom blooms during the New Year's celebration, good fortune is ahead.) String flower garlands around the room.

Another tradition during this time is giving "Lai-See envelopes." These are red envelopes that are given by senior members of the family to junior members. Each small envelope contains a small amount of money. Employers could also give red envelopes to their employees on the first working day after the festival. Give staff members token envelopes that have "school currency" in them (e.g., free lunch in the cafeteria, leave-early certificate, casual day pass).

Display the Chinese zodiac symbols: a rat, a pig, and so on. Staff members will naturally want to find out which animal they are, based on their birth year. This can make for fun discussions.

Half-Way-There Party

Celebrate the start of the second semester with a *Half-Way-There Party!* Everything about this celebration is done in halves. Send out a message inviting staff members to come *half* way through the building at *half* past the hour for some *half-*baked treats. Put a tablecloth on half of the table, cut the napkins and paper plates in half, and make half of a centerpiece. Cut cookies and small candy bars in half. Serve half cups of beverages, including coffee with half-and-half. Put out a bowl of cashew halves.

Cut the agenda or a message into halves and instruct staff members to pair up with a person who has the other half so they can read the full text. If you want to integrate a team activity into the celebration, you might distribute cards with the name of one half of a "Dynamic Duo" (e.g., "Abbott" on one card and "Costello" on another, Batman and Robin, Sonny and Cher, Cheech and Chong, The Lone Ranger and Tonto) and have each staff member find his or her partner.

Ask restaurants or retail stores to donate coupons for half off a meal or item. I'm sure you can think of a dozen more creative ideas (or at least *half* that many!) to create a fun Half-Way-There celebration.

Valentine's Day

Things I Love About My School

"Each Valentine's Day I prepare a special 'love letter' for my faculty/staff. I write one statement of admiration about EVERY person in the building. Some statements are funny, some serious, and some sentimental. Each reflects the person and my relationship with him or her. I print it on pink paper using a pretty, 'girly' font and then hand deliver them on Valentine's Day with a special, pretty cookie from a bakery. This is a huge hit! Teachers stop what they were doing to read the letter. There is no particular order to the way the names are listed, so they have to read through them to find theirs. Many share the letter with their students. It became a tradition. Some teachers and staff have kept their letters up for the whole year. One staff member even has kept every Valentine that I have ever written on her bulletin board. It takes a while to compose, but I would start a template in January and then just add to it as a thought crossed my mind."

Some examples of the things she wrote were:

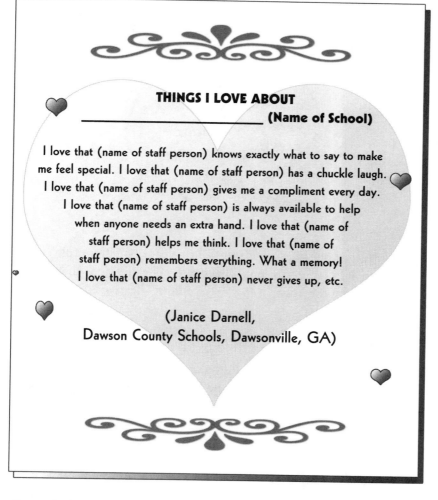

THINGS I LOVE ABOUT

_____ (Name of School)

I love that (name of staff person) knows exactly what to say to make me feel special. I love that (name of staff person) has a chuckle laugh. I love that (name of staff person) gives me a compliment every day. I love that (name of staff person) is always available to help when anyone needs an extra hand. I love that (name of staff person) helps me think. I love that (name of staff person) remembers everything. What a memory! I love that (name of staff person) never gives up, etc.

(Janice Darnell,
Dawson County Schools, Dawsonville, GA)

Flowery Praise

Give each staff member a rose and a personalized message telling why you love working with him or her.

Pass the Bouquet

Purchase a lovely bouquet of flowers, complete with a vase. Attach a Valentine greeting such as "We love working with you." Give the flowers to one staff person in the morning, but tell him or her that it can only be kept for 30 minutes. Then he or she has to give it to another staff member. The Valentine greeting circulates throughout the school at regular intervals. At the end of the day, the flowers are put in the office, staff lounge, or other location where all the staff members can enjoy them.

"Write" Valentines

Make Valentines for staff members. Buy colored markers and attach one to a construction paper heart with a message such as the following:

You are the "Write" Valentine for (Name of School)

"This year I bought pink markers. Last year I bought purple ones. Teachers look forward to seeing what color will arrive and what crazy message goes on the heart." (*Amy Estes, Sallie Gillentine Elementary School, Hollis, OK*)

Calorie Counter

Valentine's Day is symbolized by flowers and chocolates. Fill a jar with chocolate candy. Seal the jar so that no one can remove any of the candy. Give staff members slips of paper, and ask them to write down their guess as to how many calories are in the jar. The slips of paper are placed in a box nearby. This will require participants to guess how many pieces of candy are in the jar and then how many calories all of the candy would contain. The person who comes up with the exact answer or is the closest without going over the correct number is awarded the jar of candy on Valentine's Day.

Cook It With Hearts

Ask staff members to sign up to bring in food items to share with colleagues during the week of Valentine's Day. There is a bit of a catch though—the items need to be in the shape of a heart. They could be cookies, bread, finger sandwiches, and so on.

Heart-Healthy Snacks

Deviate from the traditional sweets associated with Valentine's Day. Ask staff members to sign up and bring in *heart*-healthy food items during the week. These could include fruit, low-fat yogurt, oat bran products, and so on.

Brie My Valentine

Send out invitations to staff members for a Valentine's Day event to be held after the students leave. Title it *Brie My Valentine,* and serve brie cheese, crackers, and an assortment of fruit.

Valentine's Match

Make Valentine's Day hearts in a quantity equal to half the number of people on your staff. Cut those hearts into two pieces, each in a unique way. Attach half of each heart to a sheet with the following instructional poem:

It's Valentine's Day, so what do you say
Let's get wound up and ready to play
Alone, we are an island, or so it would seem
But together we make the most wonderful team

Without others, our hearts are not whole
We need good friends to feed our soul
Attached is a heart cut in a particular way
And you must find the matching half by the end of the day

Wear your heart and you'll hopefully see
Your exact match—who will it be?
Bring both halves to the office and you'll get a treat
It won't cost you a dime and it's yummy to eat!

(Debra Macklin, Jennings Elementary School, Quincy, MI)

May this Valentine's Day be filled with love, understanding, and contentment as you journey through life with those you hold dear.

—Darly Henerson

Put one of the heart halves and a copy of the poem in each staff member's mailbox. During the day, each person has to find the staff member who has the half of the heart that matches his or hers. The pairs come to the office at the end of the day for a special treat, such as a chocolate heart candy.

Secret Valentine

A week prior to Valentine's Day, send a notice to colleagues about the *Secret Valentine* game. This notice will help you determine who's interested in participating. The poem below might accompany the notice.

Put all participants' names on slips of paper and have each person draw the name of one colleague to become that person's Secret Valentine. On the designated days, participants secretly deliver their gifts to the person whose name they drew. You could have a theme for each day as shown.

That special day is drawing near
to treat the ones we hold so dear
with something special to make them aware
how very much we really care.

This week let's try something new.
Why shouldn't we care all week through?
Let's take each day and make it unique
with a gift, a treat, or a thought written in pink.

First we'll start by drawing a name.
Then make the next five days a Valentine's game,
Each and every day leave a token
for the words so often left unspoken.

Daily Secret Valentine Themes

Day 1

Something sweet—a homemade cookie, a candy bar, or mints

Day 2

Something in the shape of a heart—a small pillow, a picture frame, or a notepad

Day 3

A heart with a message—an old-fashioned lace doily heart or a candy heart with a message on it

Day 4

A thoughtful note—Write it in pink or red ink or on pink or red paper. Mention things you appreciate about the person.

Day 5

Reveal yourself to your Secret Valentine with a small Valentine gift. (*Debra Macklin, Jennings Elementary School, Quincy, MI*)

Special Delivery

A day or two before Valentine's Day, provide all of the supplies needed to decorate heart-shaped cookies. Have staff members write special messages to their colleagues on the cookies. (If the message is too long, it can be written on a card.) Have them turn their cookies in to the person or grade-level team designated as the "cookie collector(s)." Have the person or team gather all of the cookies created for each person, package them, and deliver them on Valentine's Day.

CHAPTER 5
Sensational Spring

April Through May

PAUSE FOR APPLAUSE

Sweet Rewards

Stock up on some of the food and gum items listed. When the time is right, attach an appreciative saying to the item and give them to staff members, put them on staff members' desks, or drop them in mailboxes.

Extra Gum—Thank you for all of the *extra* help you give staff and students.

Gum—Our staff *sticks* together!

Thanks for *sticking* with us through this crazy year!

Just a **WAFER** me to say thank you for all you do.

Vanilla Wafer Cookies—Just a *wafer* me to say thank you for all you do.

Sunflower seeds—Together we are *growing* the future for our students.

Donut holes—There was a *hole* in our team while you were gone. Welcome back!

Thanks for *chipping* in to help on this project.

We appreciate what you do *a hole* bunch!

Chocolate chip cookies—Thanks for *chipping* in to help on this project.

Goldfish Crackers—The enthusiasm you show is *catching!*

Animal Crackers—This place would be a *zoo* without you!

Scoop Up the Appreciation

Seek the assistance of a local ice cream store. Put up banners that tell the staff members that they are appreciated, such as "Here is the Inside Scoop: You Are Appreciated!" Have community volunteers or the store's employees scoop and serve ice cream cones. *(Patrick O'Neill, Aiken County Career and Technical Center, Warrenville, SC)*

You could also put out the fixings for ice cream sundaes and have the staff members make their own creations. This could be a monthly event called *Sundae Monday* (or other day of the week).

Pass the Bouquet

Obtain a dozen tulips, daffodils, or other spring flowers. Give the bouquet to one staff member along with a note that expresses your appreciation for him or her. The recipient keeps one of the flowers and then passes the bouquet to the person of his or her choice with a new note.

You may want to see if local florists will periodically donate flowers so that you can do this activity throughout the year. One florist in my area gave a dozen free roses on a given day to people who agreed to keep one rose and pass the rest of the bouquet on to someone else and instruct the next person to do the same. This florist received the support of other florists to do the same and distributed more than 10,000 roses.

Tanks a Lot!

Many communities have a VFW post or other military building where tanks are on display. When the staff members have done something for which you want to extend a thank you, have a picture taken with you in front of a tank. Add the caption "*Tanks* a Lot!"

John Speeter giving "tanks"

Variation

When the staff as a group wants to extend a thank you to an individual or organization, have all of the staff members appear in the photo. Add the caption "*Tanks* a Lot!" Have them write notes of thanks under the photo. *(John Speeter, Gentiva Health Services, Kalamazoo, MI)*

Administrative Professionals Day or Week

Administrative Professionals Week, previously known as National Secretaries Week, is the last full week in April; Wednesday of that week is designated as Administrative Professionals Day. Administrative Professionals Day, Secretaries Day, My-Right-Arm Day, Super Hero Day—whatever you call it, make it a special day. Here are some ways you can give recognition to administrative assistants in your school.

A Week of Fun

Give the administrative assistants something special each day of the week. This could include a hanging flower basket, lunch at a nice restaurant, and a *You Are Worth a Million* bouquet. Change the conference or other quiet room into a spa, complete with a fountain, candles, low lights, and relaxing music—and, of course, truffles. Bring

in a massage therapist to give each administrative assistant a 20-minute foot soak or leg massage and a 10-minute chair massage. "It was very inexpensive and a big hit," says Wilma Widmer. *(Wilma Widmer, Walton County Schools, Monroe, GA)*

R-E-L-A-X

On their special day, give the administrative assistants an afternoon of pampering. Make arrangements for these staff members to have manicure or pedicure appointments. Other staff members can cover for the administrative assistants while they are enjoying their time away from the office. If there is more than one administrative assistant, it is nice if they go together to enjoy each other's company while they relax! *(Sylvia Henderson, Ross Elementary School, Milford, DE)*

If the administrative assistants are female, you could make a basket of relaxing items to use at home, such as scented candles, bath salts, spa music, body lotion, loofah mitts or sponges, and so on.

What Every Woman and Man Wants

Purchase a large basket, such as a bushel fruit basket. Prior to Administrative Professionals Day, send a memo to the staff asking each person to bring in an item for the basket that reflects the theme of *What Every Woman or Man Wants*. Fill the basket with items such as gift certificates for meals, manicures, pedicures, movies, car washes, jewelry, decorative items, magazines, books, the DVD of *What Women Want*, bubble bath, candy, gourmet coffee or tea, and so on (perhaps even auto services and self-defense classes). Present the basket to the school's administrative assistants and watch their excitement as they discover all of the gifts in the basket. Having a group gift such as this prevents hurt feelings if a staff person forgets to acknowledge the day.

Limo and Lunch

Ask staff members to contribute money for a special event for the administrative assistants in your building. Present corsages to the administrative assistants to wear for a special outing. Hire a limousine to arrive at the school and take the administrative assistants to a restaurant for lunch. Who covers the office duties? The principal, assistant principal, and parent volunteers. *(Jarcelynn Hart, Rosa Parks Elementary School, Woodbridge, VA)* You could also arrange for the limo to be stocked with sparkling grape juice to add a little more to the celebration.

It's Just What I Wanted!

Collect money from staff members to purchase gifts for the administrative assistants. To ensure that the gifts are just what they

want, the administrative assistants get to do the shopping. On Administrative Professionals Day, give each person a designated amount of money and the afternoon off. Have them go to a local shopping area and buy gifts for *themselves.* They are not to use the money for things such as groceries, items for their family, friends, or the school. The gifts have to be for themselves. At the next staff meeting, ask the administrative assistants to report to the staff, telling what they purchased. Or ask them to write a group thank-you note in which all administrative assistants describe their purchases, and have them send it to all of the staff members.

Casual Week

Give the administrative assistants a package during the week before Administrative Professionals Week. Include in the package a certificate granting them a casual day each day of that week or the following week. You could also have a button created with the message "It's Casual Administrative Professionals Week."

Ice Cream Float Celebration

Hold an Ice Cream Float Celebration in honor of the administrative assistants. Thank them for keeping things *afloat* throughout the year. You can have a nautical theme with life preservers, anchors, fish, nautical netting, and so on as decorations in order to give the room just the right feeling.

Personalize It

Give the administrative assistants personalized gifts such as business cards, notepads, a desktop nameplate, stationery, a key chain with engraved initials, or an inscribed coffee mug. You could also have a nameplate made with *Director of First Impressions* engraved on it.

Administrative assistants really are the front line of school communications!

A Flower an Hour

Put a sign-up sheet in a place where the administrative assistants won't see it. Divide the day into 60-minute increments. Staff members can sign up for one of these time slots. At the designated time, a staff member presents a single flower to each administrative assistant giving thanks for all that she or he does for the school. For example, the person could say, "Thank you for always having a smile and an encouraging word for us. You may not remember this, but earlier in the year I was really having a bad day. I came into the office to get my mail with a real attitude. You greeted me with such a smile, and you were so positive, that I left the office having had a total attitude adjustment." The first person to present the flower gives a vase at the same time. At the end of the day, the administrative assistants will have accomplished very little work but will have a vase full of flowers and received many acknowledgments of appreciation.

Variation

You can have more time slots—for example, every 15, 20, or 30 minutes someone could present a flower. Or several people could combine their time slots and make a group presentation. For example, several staff members may get together and sing a song of appreciation or read a poem they have written.

> In the age of e-mail, supercomputer power on the desktop, the Internet, and the raucous global village, attentiveness—a token of human kindness—is the greatest gift we can give someone.
>
> —*Tom Peters*

Professional Development

Typically, the administrative assistants are involved in making the arrangements for the principal, teachers, and other staff members to attend conferences. But the administrative assistants rarely get the opportunity to have a professional development day themselves. Arrange to either have speakers visit the district or county to provide training or cover expenses for administrative assistants to attend a conference or event. You can also cover the tuition costs for them to attend a class at a community college.

Ask Them!

We all change from year to year, and administrative assistants are no exception. The way in which they would like to be recognized might change annually as well. So ask the individuals how they would like to be recognized each year—do they want to attend an educational seminar, have lunch away from the school, or receive flowers, candy, gifts, gift cards, or time off? One administrative assistant e-mailed me saying that this year she asked the staff to sponsor her in a walk that raised money for cancer research—a cause very dear to her. Ask! Then they will receive exactly what they want and need.

An Administrative Assistant Does . . .

You have seen the amazing responses students give to open-ended questions such as "What does love mean?" The responses ranged from "Love is when you go out to eat and give somebody most of your French fries without making them give you any of theirs," to "Love is when your puppy licks your face even after you left him alone all day," to "Love is like a little old woman and a little old man who are still friends even after they know each other so well." These totally honest responses are darling. Have the teachers ask the students to tell what an administrative assistant does. Record their responses and submit them to one central person. Compile the best of the responses and make a display or a card to give to the administrative assistants. You could make a bulletin board for the staff lounge or office so all of the staff members can enjoy the responses.

Recognizing Noninstructional Staff Members

School Nurses

National School Nurse Day was established in 1972 to foster a better understanding of the role of school nurses in the educational setting. National School Nurse Day is celebrated on the Wednesday within National Nurse Week, which is May 6th through May 12th.

Nationwide, there are more than 60,000 school nurses who are focused on the health needs of students.

Beaded Screen

Celebrate the contributions of your school nurse by making a personalized screen for the entrance of the clinic. Paint tongue depressors in a variety of colors and carefully drill a hole in each end. (You will need to make extras because they split easily when you drill them.) Give a supply to each staff member and ask them to write a personal note of appreciation to the school nurse. Using a piece of fishing wire or dental floss, string beads and the tongue depressors together to make a vertical strand. Attach them to a dowel to make a door curtain. What a nice surprise to walk through when going to the clinic. *(Debra Macklin, Jennings Elementary School, Quincy, MI)*

Adhesive Bandage Poster

Make a poster that thanks the school nurse for his or her contributions. Integrate the bandages into the design (e.g., a nurse character made of bandages, a flower with a bandage as the center, a bandage butterfly).
(Wendy Doremus, Hudson Public Schools, Hudson, MA)

Supplies Bouquet

Instead of giving your school nurse a commercial floral bouquet, make one that is specifically for a health professional—create a bouquet out of medical supplies. You might have to raid the supply closet, but get an assortment of cotton swabs, cotton balls, alcohol swab packs, gauze, and so on. To make it look festive, add some stickers and silk greenery, and tie a bow with the gauze. This will bring a huge smile, and it doesn't need watering and won't die. *(Debra Macklin, Jennings Elementary School, Quincy, MI)*

School Nurse Serenade

Surprise your school nurse with a serenade. Using the music to "The Wanderer" (recorded by Dion), have staff members sing "The School Nurse" song. There is a section in the middle where there are no lyrics . . . just music. That's the time to put on your dancing shoes and have fun.

The School Nurse
Sung to the tune of "The Wanderer"
(4 measures of 4; 1 count to16)

Well, I'm the type of guy/gal
Who loves to be a nurse,
When a child has got a cold
and it goes from bad to worse.
When the kids are on the playground
And they're out there having fun,
I'll be standing in the clinic
where the work is never done . . .

Well, I'm the school nurse,
They call me the school nurse.
I bandage knees, and knees, and knees,
   and knees.

Well, there's bacteria and viruses—
infections everywhere,
I'm changing all the dressings
and no one seems to care.
Johnny has an earache
and feels too sick to play.
Kay needs Ampicillin,
and she needs it twice a day.

Well, I'm the school nurse,
They call me the school nurse,
I give out meds and meds and meds
   and meds.

Well, I work hard every day.
I go through life with average pay.
But I'm as happy as can be,
Seems like a million kids are waiting
to see me!

Well, I'm the type of nurse
You want to have around.
If a kid needs some help,
I always can be found.
I bandage and I treat 'em
And tell them that they're great
Then I rush 'em off to class
And say, "Now, hurry don't be late."

'Cause I'm the school nurse,
They call me the school nurse
I treat kids, and kids, and kids, and kids,
   and kids.

Musical Bridge (Your time to dance!)
(12 measures of 4; count to 4 twelve
   times)

Well, I work from sun to sun,
My job is never done.
I wouldn't trade a thing.
It's the joy that healing brings.
And if you want to know more
About who I do this for,
Just come into my clinic
And see the kids that I adore.

'Cause I'm the school nurse,
They call me the school nurse,
I run from room to room to room to room
to room.

Yes, I'm the school nurse,
I'm glad I'm the school nurse!
I answer calls, and calls, and calls,
and calls, and calls.

'Cause I'm the school nurse,
They call me the school nurse,
I take temps and temps and temps and
temps and temps.

Yes, I'm the school nurse,
They call me the school nurse . . . (fade)

I had one of the best days in my career when I was a keynote speaker at the National Association of School Nurses convention. More than 1,200 school nurses joined me in singing "The School Nurse," and some were literally dancing on their chairs. It was amazing! One school nurse, Kim Lowe from Orem, Utah, went back to her school district and revised the words to become "OSHA—The Musical." She solicited backup singers from the faculty and had them don bug antennas, which helped them get into character. Then, on the opening day of school when all the staff members had to hear about blood-borne pathogens and other annual information, she and the others performed their song. Blood-borne pathogens are pathogenic microorganisms that are present in human blood and can cause disease in human beings. These pathogens include the hepatitis B virus (HBV) and the human immunodeficiency virus (HIV). If you can find fun in the topic of germs, you can have fun with anything!

OSHA—THE MUSICAL
Sung to the tune of "The Wanderer"
(Note: There are two musical bridges in this version)

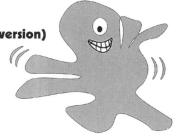

Well, we're the kind of germs
Who love to make you sick,
We live on counters and the sinks
And on the noses that are picked,
We live for weeks and don't give up,
Trying to make you sick!
Hep A, Hep B, and HIV,
We really are a kick!

We're the wanderers,
Yes, the wanderers,
We pass round and round and round
and round!

Well, there's bacteria and viruses,
Infections everywhere.
Just try to avoid us
We give you all that dare!
We're so small you can't see us
Yet we are always there
You get fever and the chills
And rashes everywhere!

We're the wanderers,
Yes, the wanderers,
We pass round and round and round
and round!

Musical Bridge (Your time to dance!)
(12 measures of 4; count to 4 twelve times)

Universal precautions,
We think they really suck,
If you use them every day,
We're fresh out of luck!
Hand washing and gloves,
And sometimes goggles, too
They make infecting you
A chore that's hard to do!

We're the wanderers,
Yes, the wanderers,

Now we're dead, we're dead,
we're dead, we're dead, we're dead!

Musical Bridge (Your time to dance again!)
(12 measures of 4; count to 4 twelve times)

Don't think that we're gone,
We're waiting here for you!
Just one little slip up
And "Ha, ha, guess who?!"
Hep A, Hep B, and HIV
We're always there for you
We're the life of the party,
In everything we do!

We're the wanderers,
Yes, the wanderers

Now we're mad, we're mad,
we're mad, we're mad, we're mad!

Cause we're the wanderers,
Yes, the wanderers,
We'll be back and back and back and back
and back!

Cause we're the wanderers,
Yes, the wanderers,
Here we are and are and are and
are and are!

Yes, the wanderers,
They call us the wanderers . . . (fade)

(Kim Lowe, Alpine School District, Orem, UT)

"What the School Nurse Does" Bulletin Board

Make a large flower to put on a bulletin board. In the center write, "The School Nurse . . ."

On each of the petals, write one of the job responsibilities of the nurse. Here are some possibilities:

- Provides emergency health care
- Delivers intervention services
- Manages acute and chronic illnesses
- Conducts health screenings
- Provides health education
- Conducts prevention programs
- Promotes environmental health and safety awareness
- Provides health counseling
- Complies with state immunization requirements
- Collaborates with school personnel, families, and the community for optimal health care
- Is a friend to students

> All work is empty save where there is love.
>
> —*Kahlil Gibran*

Praise for School Nurses

Write an opinion piece or letter to the editor for the local newspaper describing the impact that school nurses have on student success. *(Wendy Doremus, Hudson Public Schools, Hudson, MA)*

A Day in the Life

You can't totally appreciate another person's profession until you have walked in his or her shoes. Invite local officials, newspaper reporters, and so on to visit campus during School Nurse Week to view firsthand the important work that school nurses perform. *(Wendy Doremus, Hudson Public Schools, Hudson, MA)*

Instructional Aides/Paraeducators

Aides Amnesty

Provide an *Aides Amnesty* where the aides do not have to perform lunch duty on a given day. Have office staff, resource teachers, and parents cover lunch for them. During that time, the aides have a potluck luncheon with peace and quiet. *(Steve DeGaetani, Providence Elementary School, Richmond, VA)* This can be a monthly event or set aside as a special day just for aides.

Paraeducators Day

Celebrate the efforts and contributions of the paraeducational staff members by having a special lunch that honors them. Establish a theme, such as a *diner meal.* Decorate a room in diner décor and have a local restaurant cater the lunch. Play "oldies" songs such as "Rock Around the Clock," "Blue Suede Shoes," "Barbara Ann," and "Mack the Knife" in the background; show funny oldies movies. Give each person a gift and serve a special cake for dessert. "The total cost was $400 and that included the cake," shares Principal Joanne Wideman. *(Joanne Wideman, Rochester City Schools, Rochester, NY)*

Diamond Pin Paraeducators

To honor paraeducators, organize a breakfast to thank them for all of their efforts on behalf of students and staff. Give each person a "Diamond Pin" (a dime glued on to a large safety pin) as a small reminder of how valuable they are. *(Jo LeBlanc, Bear Lake Elementary School, Apopka, FL)*

Custodians

Custodians Golden Hammer Awards and Breakfast

Host a Custodians Breakfast to thank the custodians for all they have done throughout the summer and the school year. Spray paint the heads of hammers and present the *Golden Hammer Awards* to show your appreciation for their effort.

Teacher and Staff Appreciation Week

List the names of 5 people (other than your parents) who most influenced your life.

1. _____

2. _____

3. _____

4. _____

5. _____

It is likely that you have at least one teacher or other school employee on your list. Children may go a lifetime remembering a school employee who made them feel valued and special and who helped set them on a course to a fulfilling life. Educators are still helping children by challenging them to work and to dream of what can be. Organize a week to show them how much they are appreciated and what a difference they make in the lives of the students, the community, and the nation.

Teacher Appreciation Week was established by the National Education Association and National Parent Teacher Association in 1985 and takes place annually during the first full week of May. National Teacher Day is the first Tuesday of that week.

Some districts celebrate all staff appreciation events (school nurses, teachers, custodians, etc.) in one week. They designate one day of the week for an employee group, such as Monday for *Support Professional Appreciation Day*, Tuesday for *Bus Driver and School Crossing Guard Appreciation Day*, Wednesday for *Administrative Assistant Appreciation Day*, Thursday for *Custodial/Maintenance Appreciation Day*, and Friday for *Teacher and Other Professional Staff Member Day* (counselors, psychologists, social workers, school nurses, etc.). Some districts include all of the staff members in festivities for the day or weekly celebrations. Holding the celebrations all in one week promotes a team spirit.

> Every single person you meet has a sign around his or her neck that says, "Make me feel important."
>
> —*Mary Kay Ash*

Don't forget to include substitute teachers in your events. If you want them to return to your school, you will need to establish a positive relationship with them. Invite them to attend all of the events held during the week, put them on the mailing list for the district newsletter, and periodically e-mail them during the summer just to say hello. Make them feel like part of the team.

Shoot for the Stars

The recognition activities vary between districts, and they can range from small to huge events. A San Diego school incorporated theme activities into one week. The theme was *Teachers Inspire Our Children to Reach for Their Dreams and Shoot for the STARS!* They introduced the week by throwing stars in the air and sharing the theme for the week's activities.

- Classroom memory books were created.
- Pamper baskets and other treats were given throughout the week.
- A Mexican restaurant catered a lunch. A PowerPoint presentation was shown during the meal that featured the children and staff at the school and the reading of a poem written by a parent. Beverages for the event were supplied by a local grocery store.
- A local restaurant hand-delivered smoothies to the classrooms.
- A coffee establishment provided café mocha and latte espresso drinks in the staff lounge.
- Breakfast, snacks, and lunches were prepared during the week by parent chefs.
- Fifteen-minute neck and shoulder massages were offered by a chiropractic office.

- Custom imprinted stationery was given to all staff members.
- A florist helped parents create floral arrangements for each teacher.

Make It a Community Event

Many wonderful events are held in the school, but consider extending the boundaries of the recognition beyond campus. The school is a hub of community activities and events, and there are many people who would like to share in the celebration.

- Petition the local government authority to issue a special proclamation honoring school employees.
- Ask local business owners to post signs and banners; decorate their windows, billboards, and banners; and put messages on their electronic boards acknowledging the efforts of school employees.
- *We Dig Our Educators!* Ask business and community organizations to really *dig* in— get their hands dirty and sponsor the planting of a tree(s) or a flower garden in public areas or on school grounds. Put up a marker congratulating the staff from that school year.
- Ask business owners and their workers to wear pins during the week that praise school employees.
- Ask a local photographer to volunteer to take a group picture of the staff, then ask the local newspaper to publish the photo.
- Ask businesses to offer discounts on purchases made by school employees during the week.
- Have coffee shops invite school employees to stop in for a complimentary cup of coffee on their way to work.
- Invite a local reporter to spend a day as a guest teacher or other school employee and then publish the article or put the story on the air.
- Ask talk radio hosts to ask their listening audience the question, "How did a school employee affect your life?" Have community members call in and tell their stories.
- Ask your local newspapers to sell classified advertisements that honor school employees. Community members can buy space to show appreciation for all staff members or a particular school employee.
- Ask radio stations to air public service announcements that honor school employees. Most likely you will need to write these for them and give them several weeks' lead time.

These 478 staffers are all part of the success we experience at Farmingham Public Schools. Thank you all for your efforts!

- Ask a local business(es) to sponsor a schoolhouse- or apple-shaped newspaper ad that lists all the employees in the school or district. The people listed will love seeing their names—and so will their families and friends.

- Have each employee group (e.g., teachers, custodians, administrative professionals) select a person from their ranks for recognition. Design and print placemats that feature a picture of all these individuals and words of praise for these and all staff members. Distribute the placemats to restaurants throughout the community.

Staff Members Are Good Sports

Incorporate staff recognition into the sporting events that take place during Staff Appreciation Week. Some suggestions include the following:

- Have your sports announcer ask school employees to stand up to be recognized during sporting events at your school. Encourage the crowd to cheer and applaud.

- Have a special Staff Recognition Night at a home sports event in which all school employees are admitted free.

- Have the various sports teams (baseball, track, etc.) vote on a Teacher of the Week and recognize him or her at the competition held that week. Give the recipient free admission and a concession stand gift certificate. *(Tom Sharp, Oglethorpe County High School, Lexington, GA)*

For a Cause

In addition to giving gifts to staff members, or in place of gifts, sell charitable organization stars for 25 cents. Students and parents can honor staff members with stars on which the name of a staff member of their choice will be written. The stars will then be displayed at the school as a tribute to staff members. *(Debra Macklin, Jennings Elementary School, Quincy, MI)*

Tell on a Staff Member

Collect notes of appreciation from students and parents that tell what a great job a particular staff member is doing. Put the notes in a lovely basket or gift bag, or wrap ribbon around them and present them to each staff member. Make a copy and share them with the superintendent as well. These notes of praise could also be posted on the district's Web page for all to read.

Appreciation Web Page

Add a section to the district's Web page where people can write words of praise for school staff members throughout the year. You will want to have the entries screened to ensure that they are all positive. The person being written about will appreciate the entry, and coworkers and community members will read the comments and pass on the congratulations to the individuals cited when they run into them around town—doubling the treat!

Staff Member Appreciation

This section of the _____ School District Web page is dedicated to the positive efforts put forth by all of our staff. Please feel free to enter comments about a particular staff member who has made a difference in a life. If you have pictures, they are welcome as well.

Staff Person: Fran Rosenthal
Occupation: Bus Driver
Submitted by (Parent): William Brown

Fran Rosenthal is an amazing person. First of all, I can't imagine driving a vehicle with 54 energetic students behind me. She keeps calm and patient every day despite the weather conditions that living in the Midwest creates. She is the bright spot of each student's day as she greets them with a smile and welcomes them by name. No matter how the day has started for them, it is a good day when they get on the bus. She is the first and last school person in their school days, and each day is filled with care and compassion. I am grateful for all she is doing for our children.

Staff Person: James Turner
Occupation: High School English Teacher
Submitted by (Former Student): Sally Timmer

Mr. Turner's voice has never left my head in all of these years. I work in a hospital, and every time I hear someone say, "Lay down" to a patient, I want to correct them. I can hear Mr. Turner saying . . . "Lay means to put or place. Lie means to rest or recline." Who would have guessed that his words would have a lasting impact? And "We don't get *mad* at people, we get *angry*." His words live on in me!

Motivational Quotes

Each day, include motivational quotes about education on banners and posters throughout the school. Read inspirational quotes during the morning announcements. Give each staff person a notepad that has quotes on each page. Write personalized notes and include a quote to remind staff members how important they are. These are also great to put into customized fortune cookies. A good resource for quotes is the book, *Quote This!* (www.corwin.com).

Daily Gifts

Many schools present staff members with small tokens of appreciation each day, such as bookmarks, video rental certificates, academic calendars, candles, car wash certificates, movie passes, personalized pencils and notepads, prepaid phone cards, ice cream certificates, balloons, key chains, plants, bookmarks, T-shirts, candy, tote bags, memo pads, plants, and so on.

Look in the Mirror—Who Do You See?

Purchase small mirrors at variety shops, such as discount stores. Attach a note on each one that says, "You are looking at one brilliant teacher (or other job title)." Place the mirror at the workstation of each staff member before they arrive in the morning. *(Tammy Richter, New Holstein Elementary School, New Holstein, WI)*

Supplies Party

Ask parents, community members, vendors, and so on to contribute materials that can be used in the classrooms and offices, such as posters, high-quality chalk, books, games, holiday decorations, pencils, notebooks, notepads, and other supplies. Package these and have a surprise *Supplies Party* for the school employees.

Out to Lunch

When I worked in the schools, I felt like Goldie Hawn in the movie *Private Benjamin.* "Where are the condos? I want to go out to lunch!" I wanted to go out to lunch—a real lunch that was in a restaurant, was without students or lunch duty, and that lasted longer than the allocated 22 minutes. I wanted a lunch hour, not a "lunch moment."

McHenry Elementary School has the solution. During Staff Appreciation Week, they have parents supervise the classrooms from 11:00 a.m. to 1:00 p.m. so that staff members can go to lunch and have a massage—compliments of the *Cheer Committee. (Robert Graham, McHenry Elementary School, Radford, VA)*

Dinner Is on Us!

One of the most appreciated gifts is to not have to go home after work and make dinner. For the day or the week, give staff members a dinner break. Seek assistance from community and parent volunteers to prepare homemade dinners that staff members can simply heat and eat. Dinner ideas might be lasagna, chili, or casseroles. Be sure they are packaged in disposable packaging so staff members don't have to worry about returning bowls and dishes. Don't forget to include heating instructions with the item. You could also arrange for pizza delivery or give take-out restaurant coupons for a dinner for the whole family.

Pick-a-Prize Auction

Obtain gifts from parents, community members, and vendors. These could be theme baskets, gift certificates, or products. Put a sealed can with a slot in front of each item to be auctioned. Each day of the week, give all staff members a few raffle tickets. Instruct each person to write his or her name on the tickets and place them in the cans that correspond with gifts they would like to win. On Friday, draw a ticket from each can and announce the winners of each gift.

Daily Theme Celebration

Pick a different theme for each day of the week, and give staff members corresponding gifts. An example could be:

Monday—*Nature Day* (flowers, veggies, etc.)

Tuesday—*Sweets Day* (or *Baked Goods Day*)

Wednesday—*Relaxation Day* (or *Pampered Day*)

Thursday—*Thankful Thursday:* anything with *thanks* in it

Friday—*Gift Day*

Other days—*Bagel Day* and *Gourmet Coffee Day*

> I praise loudly. I blame softly.
>
> —Catherine the Great

Gifts From Parents and Students

A Treat a Day

You can involve students and parents in recognizing staff members. Well in advance of Staff Recognition Week, send a notice to the parents.

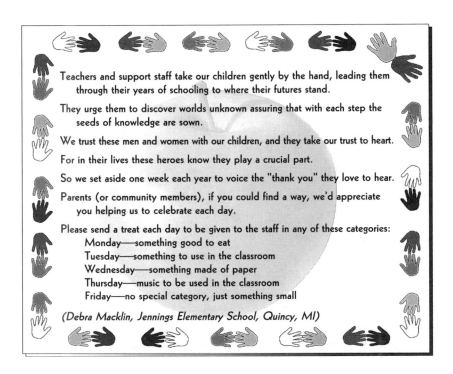

Teachers and support staff take our children gently by the hand, leading them through their years of schooling to where their futures stand.

They urge them to discover worlds unknown assuring that with each step the seeds of knowledge are sown.

We trust these men and women with our children, and they take our trust to heart.

For in their lives these heroes know they play a crucial part.

So we set aside one week each year to voice the "thank you" they love to hear.

Parents (or community members), if you could find a way, we'd appreciate you helping us to celebrate each day.

Please send a treat each day to be given to the staff in any of these categories:
Monday—something good to eat
Tuesday—something to use in the classroom
Wednesday—something made of paper
Thursday—music to be used in the classroom
Friday—no special category, just something small

(Debra Macklin, Jennings Elementary School, Quincy, MI)

Thirst Quencher

Have students, such as those enrolled in an educational career pathway, give teachers a recognition gift. Have them attach a note with a rubber band to a bottle of water that says, "You quench our thirst for knowledge." Deliver the water to department heads or put them in the teachers' mailboxes. *(Mary Lykens, Delaware Area Career Center, Delaware, OH and Crissy Lauterbach, Butler Tech-Lakota East High School, Liberty, OH)*

Tea Break

Supply the staff lounge with gourmet teas. Put notes on the tea that incorporate the use of the word *tea*. Some examples include:

Our staff is *tea*-rrific!

We appreciate your creativi–*tea* more than you know.

Have a break and enjoy the tranquili–*tea.*

Your generosi–*tea* toward students is appreciated!

Take a break and enjoy the simplici–*tea* of a warm drink.

This is said with all sinceri–*tea:* "Our staff is great!"

You can also host an afterschool tea party in which you serve tea sandwiches and cookies.

Our Staff Shines!

Have parent volunteers come to the school and polish the staff members' shoes. Advertise the event by using the slogan *Our Staff Shines!* and have signs displayed where the volunteers are stationed.

We Appreciate You S'more and S'more!

You never outgrow the great taste and gooey texture of s'mores. Most people first learn about s'mores on a camping trip, where they are made by piercing marshmallows with a stick and toasting them over a campfire. Often, more marshmallows end up in the fire than on the graham crackers, but it's great fun anyway. It's hard to replicate a campfire in the school setting, so have indoor s'mores using a microwave instead. You could decorate the room with campsite décor (such as tents and backpacks) and have the staff members wear outdoor-type clothing (such as flannel shirts, bandanas, hiking boots, and safari hats). Serve beverages in tin cups. Have a sing-along with campfire songs.

Indoor S'mores (Serves 4)

4 graham crackers, broken into halves
2 milk chocolate bars, broken into halves
4 marshmallows

Place graham cracker half on a paper towel.
Top with chocolate bar half and a marshmallow.
Microwave on medium (50%) in 10-second intervals until marshmallow puffs.

Immediately top with remaining graham cracker half; gently press together.
Serve immediately.

(Continued)

You Mean the World to Us!

The students who attend our schools represent an array of nationalities and cultures—and also, therefore, foods. Host a staff luncheon that features the international theme. Involve parent groups or local ethnic restaurants to help create and serve a lunch buffet of international foods. Place the country's flag in front of each dish and make a small sign that identifies each food item. Ask the volunteers to provide the recipe in advance and compile a cookbook titled *You Mean the World to Us!* for each staff member. Parent volunteers can also dress in clothing typical for their country. Display travel posters around the room and play international music to help set the mood and the theme of the celebration. Hang a U.S. map and world map on the wall, and ask each staff member to mark where he or she was born.

Variation

Using the international theme, have a different country represented at a luncheon each day of the week. The theme might be *A World of Thanks* or *Around the World in 182 Days*. For example, Monday's menu might call for Chinese food, Tuesday's menu for Italian, and so on. You could give staff members a weekly "plane ticket" with stops each day at the country being represented. Have hosts serve as flight attendants who greet staff at the door and say good-bye to them when they leave.

Note: You may need to arrange for classrooms to be covered so that all the staff can eat together at one time and for an extended period of time. Often, this is one of the few times that staff members get a duty-free, relaxing lunch where they can all eat together as a group.

A Mexican Vacation

Set the theme for the celebration as a *Day in the Sun—A Mexican Vacation.* Decorate with backdrops that depict Mexican culture and the country's natural scenery (such as deserts, seas, and beaches). Feature Mexican food (such as guacamole, tacos, salsa and chips, rice, and beans) and music. Highlight the event with a shopping spree. Give each person play money to represent 10 pesos, which can be used to purchase an inexpensive appreciation gift. Have a display of gifts such as beads, baskets, paper flowers, and pottery from which staff members can choose their own gift.

We Have Flipped Over Our Staff!

Flip-flops are the theme for this staff appreciation event. You can give staff members little mementos throughout the week, such as flip-flop magnets on cards that say, "We have flipped over our staff." You may be able to either find notepads with images of flip-flops on them or make up a set of your own.

Encourage students to wear flip-flops on a designated day, and give staff members a pair as a gift. (You will need to know their shoe sizes in advance.) Have a festive summer celebration that features summer foods such as lemonade, popsicles, hot dogs, and so on, and have summer music playing in the background.

Working Together Is Paradise!

Set a festive, tropical theme for the week. Encourage staff members to wear tropical clothing that reflects the theme—flowered shirts and dresses, straw hats, and so on. Decorate the staff lounge with palm trees, parrots, and tiki lights. Have daily drawings and award the winners with tropical items such as a pineapple, flamingo items, and other fun, inexpensive prizes.

Decorate a cart with fresh fruit and summer beverages, such as tropical punch and lemonade. After the students have left for the day, go to the various classrooms and serve staff members a tropical treat.

Host a festive staff gathering that continues the theme. Dress up the lounge with summer décor and give each person a lei when he or she enters. Serve tropical fruit smoothies to everyone—and be sure to put the little umbrella in the glass!

Our Staff Is Scent-sational!

Organize a week that is filled with a myriad of special scents. Have hot, homemade bread waiting for the staff members when they arrive in the morning. Be sure to have peanut butter, jams, jellies, and butter available. Don't skimp . . . make it real butter! Have fresh, hot, just-baked *scent*-sational (or is it *sin*-sational?) chocolate chip cookies delivered for an afternoon treat. Note: If you want some sinfully delicious cookies, you can order them from Sinsational Cookie (www.sinsationalcookie.com). The company is owned and operated by a retired English teacher in Michigan.

Each day, give staff members gifts such as candles, lotions, or bath salts. Ask a local store or spa to have one of their employees visit the school and host a *scent*-sational foot massage event. After the students leave, invite staff members to give themselves a stress-relieving foot massage with a variety of scented lotions.

We Love You Tender

Show your staff members how much you love and appreciate them by inviting them to an Elvis luncheon. The invitation can say something like the following:

YOU ARE INVITED TO A
We *Love You Tender* Luncheon

Join us for
Fried Peanut Butter and Banana Sandwiches
and
Chicken Tenders

Decorate with Elvis memorabilia, play Elvis music, and have a guest appearance by an Elvis look-alike. You can also borrow or rent an Elvis costume and be the star. Such fun! *(Cathy Ramsey and Dan Cox, Reagan Elementary School, Rogers, AR)*

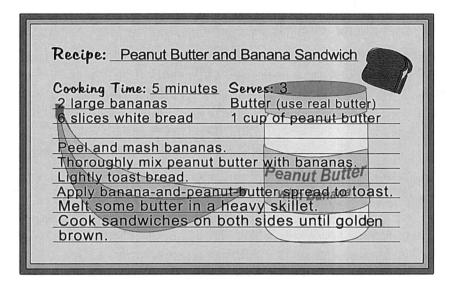

Recipe: Peanut Butter and Banana Sandwich

Cooking Time: 5 minutes **Serves:** 3

2 large bananas   Butter (use real butter)
6 slices white bread   1 cup of peanut butter

Peel and mash bananas.
Thoroughly mix peanut butter with bananas.
Lightly toast bread.
Apply banana-and-peanut-butter spread to toast.
Melt some butter in a heavy skillet.
Cook sandwiches on both sides until golden brown.

You could also have the staff compete in an *Elvis Soundalike Contest* to see who does the best Elvis impersonation.

Stress Down Week

Make the week a stress-relieving period. Announce the theme a few days beforehand and include some details: for example, let staff members know that instead of casual dress day, they can dress casually the entire next week. Transform the staff lounge into a spa with soft music, a trickling water fountain, and aromatherapy-type scents. Arrange for massage therapists or massage therapist students to provide 15-minute chair massages for staff members during planning or lunch times. Give daily gifts such as candles, soft music CDs, scented lotions, or manicure and pedicure gift certificates. Provide staff members with raffle tickets; the winner gets a massage at a local spa.

Our Staff Is Incredi-bowl!

Use the word *bowl* to create celebrations. You could plan a bowling party for staff members. Refer to Chapter 2 for ideas on how to plan a fun bowling event.

You could invite staff members to meet for an informal breakfast featuring, of course, bowls of cereal and oatmeal.

You could also have a soup buffet lunch and serve bowls of soup for the staff members. Use "Our staff is *soup*-er" on displays and invitations.

The bowls could also be used with other treats served after the students leave, such as bowls of ice cream or popcorn.

Our Staff Is Write On!

Use a writing theme for the staff celebration. Purchase or make notepads with inspirational sayings or educational humor on each page. Give them as a gift to each staff member with a note that says, "Our staff is *write* on!" or "Our staff has the *write* stuff!" These make nice gifts; the motivational sayings and fun get passed around among staff members long after the week is over. You could also have personalized notepads (with "From the desk of . . ." at the top) made for each staff member. People who like to see their names in print especially appreciate these. (Thought pads with inspirational quotes are available from Positive Promotions www.positivepromotions.com.)

Place an advertisement in the newspaper that lists all of the staff members' names on a notepad, and use the designated theme. Host a luncheon and cover the tables with sign paper. Provide crayons and markers and encourage staff members to write on the table covering.

You Are Kneaded

Forget the no- and low-carbohydrate diets—this day is full of carbs! Have bread machines going early in the morning so the aroma will permeate the school. Make fresh bread for the staff members to enjoy during their breaks and lunch. Offer an assortment of jams, jellies, peanut butter, and butter. Hang a *You Are Kneaded!* sign or banner above the treats.

Our Staff Is Magical!

Each day, e-mail a magic trick to each staff member. You can find these on YouTube and on the Web pages of magicians such as David Copperfield. Host a staff luncheon and play songs featuring the word *magic*. Such music might be "Magic" by The Cars, "Do You Believe in Magic" by The Lovin' Spoonful, "You Can Do Magic" by America, and "Could It Be Magic" by Barry Manilow. Find a local magician to provide entertainment during the lunch. Serve rabbit-shaped cake. Make a large top hat display from which you pull out gifts for each staff member. Let the children get in on the excitement, too, by having the magician visit classrooms.

We Are Lucky to Have You!

Purchase a lucky bamboo plant for each staff member. Attach a card to it and deliver it personally, telling each person why the school is lucky to have him or her on staff.

You could also incorporate the four-leaf clover into the celebration. Make a four-leaf clover cutout for each person. On each of the leaves, write a quality that the individual displays. For example, "We are *lucky* to have you on staff because . . . you are always willing to help your coworkers" or " . . . you show such patience with students." Make the qualities specific to the recipient. This item will be kept for a long time.

Our Staff Has Class!

Incorporate a classical music theme into a staff luncheon. During the morning, have a classical guitarist or violinist serenade staff members in their classrooms, workrooms, when the busses arrive, and so on. Have the school's chamber music orchestra or a community group play during lunch.

Our Staff Blooms!

Use a floral and garden theme throughout the week. Decorate the staff lounge with paper flowers, use floral paper plates when serving treats, and so on. Fill clay pots wrapped in ribbon with candy, and place them in the staff lounge or in the office. For staff gifts, give candles in the shape of flowers, floral picture frames or notepaper, or packets of flower or vegetable seeds. Use inspirational sayings such as, "Thank you for helping our children bloom." If you are serving lunch, you may want to make a garden theme and have vegetable lasagna or a large salad bar.

Our Staff Is Way Cool!

Cool is the theme for the week. Prepare a cart of lemonade and iced tea, and serve it to staff members at their workstations. After the students leave for the day, have a sundae social and provide all of the fixings for staff members to create their own ice cream sundaes. Have blenders available and make smoothies for the staff members during their planning periods and breaks. If you are serving lunch, make all the food items *cool*—offer items such as a salad bar, sandwich bar, and cool soups. Serve gelatin and pie topped with Cool Whip.

Our Staff Is On Course

Plan a staff outing to a golf course or a miniature golf course. Or transform the school's gym or cafeteria into a golf course and invite staff members to play a few holes to help celebrate and support the idea of being "on course."

Theme Celebration

Hold a potluck luncheon sponsored by the paraeducators, custodians, and administrators. Together, select a theme, such as *Mardi Gras,* for the event. (Springfield Elementary School treated their staff to jambalaya, dirty rice, king cake, and many other dishes.) Decorate with beads and bright colors, and play jazz music. Principal Ranae Everson said, "Staff members really enjoyed their time to visit and unwind." *(Ranae Everson, Springfield Elementary School, Springfield, MN)*

Staff Lounge Makeover

Honor the staff by providing them with a nice lounge. Organize volunteers to give the room a new look with fresh paint, decorations, curtains, framed artwork, a bulletin board, and a lot of creativity. Check to see if a new microwave and refrigerator might be in order. Celebrate the completion of the revamped lounge by holding an Open House—complete with refreshments.

Staff Restrooms Makeover

To help the restroom seem less institutional, add a table with items such as hand lotion, potpourri, or scented oils. Hang nice pictures on the walls. Place an attractive wastebasket in the room. Add a small bulletin board for staff members to post notes or educational humor for others to enjoy. If the walls need a coat of paint, add it to help the room project a sense of calm.

Clean Their Rooms

With staff cutbacks, there just doesn't seem to be enough people to properly maintain classrooms. As a result, teachers are often found vacuuming and cleaning floors, dusting, and cleaning their classrooms. Gather a group of volunteers (parents, community cleaning services, business owners or employees, etc.) to clean classrooms after the students have left for the day. Coordinate this activity with your custodial staff and be sure to have cleaning supplies available in each room.

POWERED BY FUN!

Spring has sprung

The grass has risen

How many days until the end of the school year?

Staff Jeopardy

Make a Jeopardy game that reflects the staff, and play it during a long inservice day. Some of the categories could include:

- What child is this?—the answers give clues to certain students in the building
- Acronym me ASAP—which gives clues to the acronyms students use these days
- Name that tune—staff members identify either the artist or lyrics of a song
- ISMs—this reflects the "isms" that teachers use in their classrooms

"It was fun for staff to play during their lunch break from the inservice meetings. Our superintendent even came down to see what all the fun was about," noted Natalie Winkler. (*Natalie Winkler, Clear Creek Middle School, Idaho Springs, CO*)

E-mail Scrabble

Select a word such as *trap*, as shown in the example. Change one letter in the word and send the e-mail to another staff person. Ask him or her to change one letter in the word at the bottom of the list, type in his or her own name, date it, and send the e-mail to five other staff members. It will be fun to see how far the e-mail goes. To facilitate the process, you may want to include a list of staff members and their e-mail addresses in the original e-mail.

Let's Play E-mail Scrabble

Change one letter of the bottom word, and let's see how far we can make it go!

Rules:

Change only *one* letter of the word at the bottom of the list.

You cannot add letters.

You cannot use foreign languages.

Send it back to the person who sent it to you, plus five other staff members.

Cut and paste the text into a new e-mail. Add your entry to the bottom of the list and add your name and the date.

Examples:

WORD:

Trap—Sandy Baxter (date)

Trip—Maureen Napier (date)

Grip—Jack Wood (date)

Grid—Chris Baker (date)

Grin—Lyn Wood (date)

Gran—John Coombs (date)

Bran—Wendy Morris (date)

Rant—Val Parker (date)

Pant—Janet Gilboy (date)

Pint—Adriana White (date)

Punt—Laura O'Malley (date)

Puny—Sally Marion (date)

Punk—Suzan Derek (date)

Pink—Shirley Martin (date)

Sink—Harold Ford (date)

Link—Sue Hannifan (date)

Line—Denise Walton (date)

Lint—Syndey Halzelwood (date)

Tint—Evangaline Miller (date)

Spring Fling

You will need to plan for this activity in advance. At the tail end of winter, there is always a "teaser" day: the day when the temperature rises and it feels like spring. Put a note on a few Frisbees telling everyone to meet at a designated place outside after the students leave for the day. Ask staff members to fling the Frisbees to other staff members so that everyone gets the message. Have Frisbees available for everyone to toss and take home with them. You may want to have contests.

Spring Gift Exchange

Ask staff members who want to participate to bring in a wrapped spring item for a gift exchange. You can have either gag or nice gifts, or a combination of both. Some examples might include:

- Frisbee
- Flower seeds
- Spring plant
- Garden tools
- Sunblock
- Garden gloves
- Umbrella
- Potting soil
- Baseball
- Gummy Worms
- Kite
- Watering can

> Spring is nature's way of saying, "Let's party."
>
> —Robin Williams

Put all of the gifts in a pile and have the participants sit in a circle around the gifts. (If you have a large staff, you may want to create smaller groups that all meet at the same time.) Have each person select a gift but don't open them.

Create a story such as the one shown. You could incorporate the names of staff members into the story. Each time you read the words *left* or *right*, they have to pass the gift they selected to the person on their left or right. When the word *across* or *change* is read, they have to give their gift to a person sitting across the circle. When the story ends, the staff members open the gifts.

It is spring, which means there are only 30 days left in the school year. No one is really counting though, right? Who among us is not ready for the change of season? Coats being left in the closet will be a welcomed change. The weather has been bad across the country, and we are no exception. It would be nice to have some Snow Days left, but alas, we will be right here at the end of school making up days missed. We had our fingers crossed during the last snow, but it didn't work.

Mary has had an even tougher winter than most of us. She left school early, before mid-winter break and had surgery on her left knee. She came right back to work and can now be seen running across the playground with the children.

Bill would have left school yesterday on time, but one of the students needed a ride home. He left his boots at home, and it was too messy to walk. Sandy, from the office, left a message for the parents and hoped they would call right back, but they didn't. Bill had to change his plans in order to take the student across town. They left the school right before 4:00. They took a left on Main Street, a right on Hill Street, and another right on High Street before the student announced that he wasn't sure how to get to his house. They parked right across the street from the library, left the car, and went into the building to look up the address in the phone book.

(You get the gist of this, *right?* You can *change* the theme any way you want, but make sure no one is *left* out if you use names.)

Spring Planting

One sign of spring is flowers such as tulips and daffodils beginning to pop up in yards. In anticipation of spring, spread out spring flower bulbs, potting soil, flowerpots, gardening gloves, trowels, water, and so on. Encourage staff members to plant a pot for each of their classrooms so they and their students can watch for signs of spring. At the end of the year, plant the bulbs on the school grounds. You could give a prize to the person whose plant bloomed first.

"I don't care if it looks silly, I can't have my flowers getting frost bite!"

Garden Ingredients

If you live in a part of the country that has cold, snowy winters, you know how much people look forward to the coming of spring. Copy these instructions, attach a packet of flower or vegetable seeds, and give them to each staff member.

In the spring, at the end of the day, you should smell like dirt.

—Margaret Atwood

Our Garden

Plant three rows of peas.

Peas of mind
Peas of heart
Peas within yourself

Plant four rows of squash.

Squash gossip
Squash selfishness
Squash grumbling
Squash indifference

Plant three rows of lettuce.

Lettuce be kind
Lettuce listen to others
Lettuce care about each other

No garden should be without turnips.

Turnip to help one another
Turnip the music and dance

To finish our garden we must have thyme.

Thyme for fun
Thyme for rest
Thyme for family
Thyme for yourself

Water freely with patience and cultivate with love. There is much fruit in our garden because you reap what you sow.

(Adapted from original version, author unknown)

How Does Your Garden Grow?

Celebrate the arrival of spring (or its approach) by having a garden party. Here are some ideas for a very fun event:

- Make a fruit bouquet. Using skewers, pierce pineapple slices with grape centers, strawberries, and chocolate-covered strawberries and place them into Styrofoam for support. Place the bouquet into an urn for serving.
- Rent a chocolate fountain and present it with servings of angel food and sponge cake, bananas, strawberries, and so on.
- Serve the salads in all types of plastic plant pots and use shovels as spoons.
- Serve the dips in smaller pots with smaller shovels.
- Identify the contents of each dish with a small clay pot with a garden marker in it.
- Serve the nuts and mints in bird feeders.
- Serve the drinks in large watering cans with the sprinkler end removed.
- Store and serve the ice in a wheelbarrow lined with clean plastic and use a shovel for scooping.
- Serve the cutlery from small planters.
- Serve "Dirt Pudding With Worms" and decorate with apples sprouting gummy worms.
- Use garden gloves for potholders.

Note: Everything needs to be new and washed before the party. *(Debra Macklin, Quincy, MI)*

Welcome Spring!

Plan a gathering in celebration of the fact that spring has finally arrived. Bring the staff together and serve spring rolls as a treat.

Or have a Spring Luncheon in which staff members make salads and other foods that remind us that winter is over and the new season has begun. *(Mary Lou Cebula, Central School, Warren, NJ)*

Spring Cleaning

Sponsor a Spring Cleaning Clothing Swap. Have staff members bring in clothes that are in good condition; sort and display the clothes by style. Staff members can select "new" items to take home. All leftovers can be donated to charity. *(Barbara Sutterlin, Bridgewater-Rariton Regional*

School District, Bridgewater, NJ) The same could be implemented with books and toys for children.

Play Dates

Parents often plan play dates for their young children and their friends to get together. Plan play dates for the staff, too. Hold events such as the following:

- Ping-pong tournaments
- Volleyball games
- Dart competitions
- Kite flying
- Dance instruction
- Card game tournaments
- Three-on-three basketball tournaments
- Play on the playground

Baseball's Opening Day!

Baseball season is back! On opening day, encourage staff members to dress in the colors of their favorite team or wear logo attire (e.g., hats, buttons, T-shirts, socks). At lunch, serve hot dogs, potato chips, peanuts, and Cracker Jacks.

Tax Relief Day

April 15th is the dreaded income tax filing day. Take some of the sting out of the date by creating a *Tax Relief Day.* Have staff members sign up for a drawing. Make the entry forms out of simulated tax forms. At the end of the day, hold a drawing. The winner gets $10.40. (Get it? Tax form 1040.)

Or you could have a *Sweet Tax Relief Day* and serve desserts in the staff lounge or at an event after school.

Form **1040**	Department of the Treasury—Internal Revenue Service
	U.S. Individual Income Tax Return

Label			
Use the IRS label. Otherwise, please print or type.	L A B E L H E R E	Your first name and initial	Last name
		If a joint return, spouse's first name and initial	Last name
		Home address (number and street). If you have a P.O. box, see page 14.	Apt. no.
		City, town or post office, state, and ZIP code.	

Don't Tell the IRS!

Purchase money notepads and give them to staff members with a note that says, "Don't tell the IRS, but we think you are worth a million bucks!" *(Debra Macklin, Jennings Elementary School, Quincy, MI)*

Decorate Their Hats

Ask staff members to bring in an old hat or visor. Provide a workstation with decorative items such as ribbon, yarn, glue, feathers, sequins, buttons, flowers, and so on. You may want to go to a craft shop and ask them to set aside the miscellaneous items that might typically be thrown out. Staff members can also bring in decorative items of their choice. Either label each hat with the owner's name or let them be anonymous. Have each staff member select a hat or visor and decorate it. The decorators and owners match up on a specific day. Have staff members wear their spring hats to an afterschool event in which you serve lemonade and snacks.

Tie It On Day

Set a day when staff members (and students) can have a *Tie It On Day*. Participants may wear silly ties, jewelry, or boas. Staff members can wear anything they want around the neck that is silly or funny. Consider awarding prizes for the most creative tie, ugliest tie, and so on.

Jackie Townsend models her boa

70s Party (70 degrees, that is!)

When the outside thermometer hits 70 degrees, host a 70s party—a fondue fest! Serve cheese and chocolate fondue. Play classic games and have music from the 1970s in the background, songs such as "Bridge Over Troubled Water," "American Pie," "Tie a Yellow Ribbon," and "Stayin' Alive." Dressing up in the traditional John Travolta disco attire from the movie *Saturday Night Fever* is a bonus.

Delivering the Message or Prizes

Do you have a message that you need to get to your colleagues? Add some fun to it. For "ground delivery," attach the message to a remote control car and send it to the various workstations. You could also attach the message to a Frisbee if you need "air mail." This would also work for delivering prizes to winners—"express delivery."

Paper Airplane Flying

Assemble the staff outside to celebrate the first day of spring by having a paper airplane flying contest. You can find many airplane designs on the Internet. You could let staff members research their own designs and fold their own, or provide the paper and a diagram so that the airplanes are uniform. Have fly-offs until there is a winner, and then award a prize. If the weather is not conducive to doing this outside, hold the contest in the halls or in an indoor locale such as the gym or cafeteria.

A Paper Airplane

1. Fold a sheet of 8.5" × 11" paper in half lengthwise. Open up the paper, and lay it on the table with the crease up.

2. Fold the two corners until they meet at the center crease.

3. Fold each wing in half again.

4. Fold the plane sides together on the crease in the center.

5. Form the wings by folding them to the center crease on both sides.

1.

2.

3.

4.

5.

You could also tuck messages into the airplanes and then send them to colleagues.

Polka Dot Day

Plan a day when staff members (and students) are asked to wear polka dotted clothes. Send out the notice on polka dotted stationery. Sponsor an event after the students leave or put treats in the staff lounge such as Dots candy or cupcakes with dots on them.

You could also change the day to be *Plaid and Check Day* and serve Chex Mix as part of the refreshments.

Make sure you take a group photo of everyone who takes part in the event, and post the picture where staff members congregate, post it on your district's intranet, and include it in the school newsletter.

Clown Nose Day

If you have an inservice day or a day without students, have a clown nose day. Hide clown noses in areas where the staff members congregate. Have them search for the noses, and when they are found, the person gets to wear the nose for an hour.

Who Made This?

Have staff members bring in food items for a potluck luncheon. Put all of the prepared dishes (keeping their creators anonymous) on a decorated table. Place a number by each food item. Give each staff member a piece of paper with the participating staff members' names and food item numbers on it. Have them guess who made each dish. The person with the correct answers or the most number of correct answers is the winner. The winner gets an extra dessert or the opportunity to lead the group through the buffet line.

"Chef" Gerry Martin

Spring Fever Lunch

After that teaser day, when you realize you actually have days, weeks, or even months of winter still ahead, hold a *Spring Fever Lunch*. Cover the tables with brightly colored checkered tablecloths and accent them with flowers in watering cans. Decorate with butterfly- and bee-shaped sugar cookies.

Provide fun toys, such as jump ropes and jacks. Have an indoor corn toss. Divide the staff members into teams of two and give each team an ear of corn. The rules are simple: players have to (1) catch the corn and (2) take a step back each time they toss the corn to their partner. The team to catch their corn from the farthest distance is the winner. Give the winning team a gift with a springtime theme.

Spring Tailgate Party

At lunch, hold a tailgate party in the parking lot to celebrate the ability to go outside and enjoy the good weather again. Serve garden burgers and a salad. (You might want to make sunflower seeds available too.) Decorate with flowers, gummy worms, and so on.

Principal Kathy Lina and her administrative assistant host an annual tailgate party. They bring their barbecue grills from home and cook hamburgers, hot dogs, and sausage. Tables are set up outdoors for all staff members (instructional, bus drivers, maintenance, etc.) to enjoy some fun time outside. Dessert is also provided. "The total cost for the event is less than $200, and the Activity Fund is used and/or the PTO helps with the cost," said Kathy Lina. *(Kathy Lina, Lorena Independent School District, Lorena, TX)*

Garden Lunch

Host a garden lunch that features a variety of salads. If the weather is conducive to eating outside, make it a picnic. If not, transform your area into a spring environment by using flowers, butterflies, ladybugs, and so on as decorations. As table favors, give each person a packet of flower seeds.

Bake My Day

Play off the line made famous by Clint Eastwood's character, Inspector ("Dirty") Harry Callahan, in the 1983 film *Sudden Impact:* "Make my day." Change it to *Bake My Day* and have baked goods available for the staff members to enjoy. Set up tables of goodies, including cupcakes, cookies, pie, and cake. Yum! (FYI: Dirty Harry wasn't the first to use the phrase with that meaning. It had been spoken earlier by Tom Walsh, a character in the 1982 film *Vice Squad*.)

Pie on the Fly

When the staff members have a particularly busy week and a get-together is just out of the question, invite them to have a piece of pie "on the fly." Have pies located in a communal spot, such as the staff lounge, office, or copy room. Invite the busy staff members to take a piece of pie with them when they get a chance.

SPRING CELEBRATIONS

Easter

Egg-citing Rewards

Take this opportunity to give staff members a candy egg with an *egg*-citing note attached.

> You are an *EGG*-ceptional staff member!

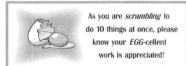

> As you are *scrambling* to do 10 things at once, please know your *EGG*-cellent work is appreciated!

You are an *egg*-ceptional staff member!

Students really get *egg*-cited when you teach.

You are an *egg*-cellent staff member.

As you are *scrambling* to do 10 things at once, please know that your *egg*-cellent work is appreciated!

Hat Day

In years gone by, Easter parades in which people wore new springtime clothes and hats were popular. Irving Berlin wrote about the New York festival with the following words:

> In your Easter bonnet
>
> with all the frills upon it,
>
> You'll be the grandest lady in the Easter parade.

Marc Hodges

Have your own hat celebration. Ask staff members to take pictures of themselves wearing a hat, and then post them on the intranet or on a bulletin board in the staff lounge. Throughout the week, have the staff members vote for the winners in categories such as *Funniest, Most Attractive,* or *Most Creative.* On the last day, have a gathering and announce the winners. You could ask everyone to wear their hats to the event. Serve a hat-shaped cake and award the prizes.

Egg-citing Search

While staff members are out of the building, visit their classrooms or workstations. Hide plastic eggs filled with candy and an Easter greeting for them to find. Stamp some of the messages with a star or a smile. The people who get these stamped eggs receive a special gift appropriate for the holiday. Put the following poem in a visible spot so everyone can read about the event. *(Debra Macklin, Jennings Elementary School, Quincy, MI)*

There is no Easter Bunny, some silly people say.
No bunny can lay all of those eggs in a day.

But we say "phooey" to those who would doubt.
We know he exists. And though we've not heard him shout
We have found some *egg*-citing clues hidden about.

If you look around, you are sure to find
An egg of the most interesting kind.
It could be hidden anywhere in your space.
It might even be in an obvious place.

Inside is a message that will be found
And something sweet that weighs less than a pound.

If your message is stamped with a smile or a star
Dash down to the office, you don't need a car.

When you get there you will be allowed to choose
A fabulous gift—you see—you can't lose!

Happy Easter!

Caption It!

Collect cartoons or pictures that relate to Easter, such as the one shown. Remove any captions and text that may go with the pictures. Send the cartoons to the staff and ask them to write captions for the pictures.

Post each picture or cartoon on a big sheet of shelf paper with plenty of extra room for writing. Have a supply of markers handy so that staff members can write in their captions. You can either have staff members identify their captions or have them be anonymous. You could make a contest out of it and have staff members vote for the best captions.

Cinco de Mayo

Cinco de Mayo is the day used to celebrate the Battle of Puebla that occurred on May 5, 1862, in which the Mexican Army defeated the French Army. Although the holiday is often confused in the United States with the Mexican Independence, Mexico's independence from Spain was actually declared on September 16, 1810. Both holidays are times to celebrate the rich culture of Mexico.

Fiesta Olé!

Send staff members colorful invitations to the fiesta, and decorate the announcements with pictures of the

Mexican flag and so on. Transform the lounge or cafeteria into a colorful fiesta site. Decorate with chili pepper wreaths and incorporate the colors of the Mexican flag (red, white, and green) into the decorations through balloons, raffia to tie the napkins, and plates and cups. Mexican serape blankets make great tablecloths or wall hangings.

Set up a taco buffet with heaping bowls of scrumptious fillings. Also include chili con queso, chicken lime soup, guacamole and chips, salsa, pinto beans, Mexican rice, and flan. Play Mexican music during the meal.

You could also bring in a quesadilla maker and prepare quesadillas for the staff members as a meal or as an afterschool treat. *(Carol Kahler, Gilbert Linkous Elementary School, Blacksburg, VA)*

Salsa Contest

Hold a Salsa Contest as part of the fiesta. Each person prepares his or her favorite recipe for the other staff members to sample. Have a large supply of tortilla chips available. Ask for volunteers to serve as judges to select the winners of various categories such as *mild, medium, hot,* and *fire!* Have each participant make copies of his or her recipe to share with colleagues.

CHAPTER 6
End of the School Year
Ahhh Summer!

REFLECTION

A Year in Review

At the beginning of the year, give everyone a disposable camera to capture the events that happen during the subsequent months. Compile them into a DVD, scrapbook, or bulletin. Reflect on the year's successes, fun, and learning.

Variation

Make a "Year in Review" booklet that displays pictures and lists or describes achievements. Celebrate the journey of getting to where you are.

1:1 Meeting

At the end of the school year, the principal schedules a 10- to 15-minute meeting with each staff member (complete with snacks). Praise, kudos, and compliments are given for specific actions that the staff member performed during the year. *(Kristi Griffith, Grandview Intermediate School, Grandview, TX)*

Picture Your Year

Give each staff member a piece of newsprint and a marker and ask him or her to describe the year. Allow each person time to share reflections, successes, learning experiences, adventures, and laughs. If you have a large staff, divide them into smaller groups. The year could also be described in another way, such as through a picture, song, or skit.

PAUSE FOR APPLAUSE

Thanks a *Latte*

It's the end of the year, and you want to thank everyone for a job well done. Obtain latte machines and say thanks a *latte* by making a variety of lattes for the staff members. Serve biscotti, scones, or other treats as well.

Signing Bonus

Each year, the district sends a letter of intent to rehire staff members. At Edison Elementary School, in Kennewick, Washington, Principal Bruce Cannard takes the letters to the staff members and asks if they would be willing to join the team for another year. He indicates that if they "re-up" they will receive a significant signing bonus.

The signing bonus is a large Hershey candy bar wrapped in a paper that describes the other perks of the job. Bruce Cannard shared, "I made a list of things that will come to them in the coming year if they sign on that were just for laughs." (e.g., "Eager children will hang on your every word.") *(Bruce Cannard, Edison Elementary School, Kennewick, WA)*

End-of-the-Year Celebration and Awards

Host a Victory Party to celebrate the accomplishments of the year. The event could be a major event, such as a picnic or a potluck. However you plan it, the year needs to be celebrated. You might include a chorus, speaker, luncheon, or a media presentation of the year. As part of the event, give certificates to staff members based on achievement or personality traits. Prepare ballots with the various awards and a description of each award that is listed. Have staff members vote on who should be awarded the certificate. To add an extra element of fun, read the description of the award aloud and let the staff members guess who the recipient will be.

Most Willing to Help a Team Member Award

The person who always says "yes" when help is needed

Most Positive Attitude Award

The person who always has a positive attitude and shares it with those around him or her

After-Hours Award

The staff member who is most likely to be found working after hours

School Spirit Award

The person who shows the most school spirit

Cheerleader Award (give pom-poms)

The person who is always cheering on new initiatives and ideas

Adhesive Award (give a bottle of glue)

The person who held everyone together throughout the year

Johnny Appleseed Award

The person who plants the seeds of happiness

Rookie of the Year Award

A new staff person who excelled at the new job

Extra Mile Award

The person who always goes above and beyond expectations

> The way to develop the best that is in a person is by appreciation and encouragement.
>
> —*Charles Schwab*

Toast to a Successful Year

Just as the start of the year is a celebration, so too should the end of the year be celebrated. So much has been accomplished that everyone should reflect on the success of the year and set goals for the following year. If you set a theme for the year (Chapter 2), then carry that theme through to the ending celebration. If you didn't have a theme, then have a *Toast to a Successful Year*.

Invite the staff to an event, have good-bye songs playing as they enter—for example, "Happy Trails" by Dale Evans, "See You Later Alligator" by Bill Haley and His Comets, "Na Na Hey Hey Kiss Him Goodbye" by Steam, "So Long, Farewell" from *The Sound of Music*, or "School's Out" by Alice Cooper.

Serve sparkling grape juice in champagne glasses (glass, not plastic). Serve a celebratory cake with a motivational message written on it. Make sure all staff members get the chance to make a toast if they want to.

The Jimmys (The Oscars)

To show staff appreciation, have your own version of the Academy Awards ("the Oscars") Ceremony. Develop some creative categories to honor staff members, such as the following:

- Best Dressed
- Best Decorated Room
- Best Person of Character
- Social Butterfly
- Biggest Joker
- Principal's Pet
- Most Use of Technology in the Classroom
- Teacher Who Stays the Latest
- Teacher Who Leaves the Earliest
- Teacher Who Arrives the Earliest
- Teacher Who Arrives the Latest
- Best Curriculum Meeting Coordinator
- Biggest Coffee Consumer
- Biggest Consumer of Paper
- Best Halloween Costume
- Best Coordination of Wardrobe With Curriculum
- Most Energetic in the Morning

Nominations

Give each faculty member a nominee ballot with the list of categories. They may make a note or comment in addition to casting their votes. Tabulate the votes and take staged pictures of the three people who received the most nominations in each category. Principal Jim Mule commented, "We had fun taking the staged pictures. For example, the finalists for the Principal's Pet Award had pictures taken with one teacher shining my shoes, one cutting my hair, and one serving me coffee."

Official Ballot

List the names of the three staff members who received the most nominations in each category. Staff members may vote for one person in each category.

Awards Dinner

Create a PowerPoint presentation to show at a teacher appreciation dinner. Include slides that announce the category, "The nominees are . . ." and "The winner is. . . ."

> There is nothing I need so much as nourishment for my self-esteem.
>
> —*Alfred Lunt*

The winner of each category is called to the podium to receive the award—a gift certificate. The awards may be titled after the principal. (In this case, "The Jimmys" were the name of the awards.) *(Jim Mule, St. Amelia School, Tonawanda, NY)*

The Wizard of Oz Awards

At the end of the year, have a Wizard of Oz celebration. Have staff members vote on which of their colleagues will receive awards that correspond to the characters in the story.

- The Big Heart Award
- The Welcoming Home Award
- The Brainy Smart Award
- The Courage Award
- The Good Witch Award
- The We Aren't in Kansas Anymore, ToTo Award

Smoothie Party

Invite staff members to celebrate the completion of a *smooth year*. Talk about the good things that happened during the year, and serve smoothies as refreshment.

Admission by Ticket Only

Ask each staff member to submit a positive achievement they accomplished during the year and that they are proud of. When they submit their achievement, they are given a ticket to attend an end-of-the-year celebration. At the event, read each person's achievement. Have the group applaud each other's accomplishments. Encourage the applause to get louder and louder so that people are cheering, whistling, whooping, and hollering! It will be a positive surge of energy and a sense of satisfaction that will carry over to the start of the school year.

POWERED BY FUN!

We Are the Champions!

End the year by having a fun group event: Staff Olympics. Organize several lighthearted games in which staff members compete. Some events might include the following:

Broom Baseball

Use a broom instead of a bat and run the bases backward.

A Day at the Beach

Give each team a beach chair and a bag that contains beach items such as a towel, sunglasses, sunblock, and a book. To begin the event, one person from each team picks up the items and carries them to the finish line. There, he or she spreads out the towel, sets up and sits in the beach chair, applies sunblock, puts on the sunglasses, and opens the book. After finding comfort at the beach, he or she reverses the process by repacking the book, sunglasses, towel, and sunblock into the beach bag and folding up the chair. The staff member runs back to the team and hands off the items to the second team member, and so on. The team with the fastest time wins.

Dress-Up Relay

Fill two backpacks with oversized school clothing such as a baseball cap, shirt, shorts, shoes, and a belt. Organize the staff members into teams. Have the first person on each team race to a designated spot with the backpack in hand, open it, and put each of the clothing items on over his or her own clothes. When the staff member is fully dressed, he or she then takes off each item, repacks the backpack, and runs back to the team. He or she hands off the backpack to the next team member and the relay continues. The team that finishes the fastest wins.

Find the Rainbow

Divide the staff members into teams. Give each team a bag with a piece of paper with the colors of the rainbow (red, orange, yellow, green, blue, indigo, and violet) written on it. Instruct each team to find and put in the bag an object from outside that matches each color. The winner is the first team to find objects that match all of the colors.

Foot Golf

Set a golf course up around the school. Play a game of golf where staff members have to kick the ball rather than hit it with a golf club.

If the Shoe Fits

Divide the staff members into teams. Each staff member removes one shoe and puts it in one big pile. At the start of the game, one person from each team runs to the pile of shoes, finds his or her shoe, and returns to the team. The competition continues until all the staff members have returned to the line. The team that finishes first wins.

Hula-Hoop Relay

Divide the staff members into an even number of teams, and provide a hula hoop and a stick for each team. Devise a course for each team to follow. Start the relay by blowing the whistle; then each competitor rolls the hoop through the course and back by using either a hand or the stick. The hula hoop is handed off to the next player. The relay continues until all of the players of one team complete the course.

Staff Meeting Sing-Along

At the last staff meeting of the year, have a staff sing-along and encourage people to bring thoughts of summer into the room. Here is a delightful song to help put summer in the thought process—as if you need help to get your minds there!

Oh, My Summer

(To the tune of "Oh My Darling, Clementine")

In a building, in a classroom,
I've been teaching every day,
But the tank now, it's on empty,
I've got nothing left to say.

Oh, my summer, oh, my summer,
Oh, my summer's finally here.
There were times I didn't know if
I would make it through the year.

No more classes, no more meetings,
No more kids to entertain,
No more donuts for my homeroom,
No more parents who complain.

Oh, my summer, oh, my summer,
Oh, my summer's finally here.
There were times I didn't know if
I would make it through the year.

Wrote my comments on my laptop.
I've had such computer woes.
Looked around, but never found them,
Didn't save before it froze.

Oh, my summer, oh, my summer,
Oh, my summer's finally here.
There were times I didn't know if
I would make it through the year.

These were lean years for some seniors,
Always turned their work in late,
Didn't know if they would make it
To the stage to graduate.

Oh, my summer, oh, my summer,
Oh, my summer's finally here.
There were times I didn't know if
I would make it through the year.

Oh, it's not that I don't love them.
Oh, I absolutely do.
But I'm tired, uninspired,
And I need a month or two.

Oh, my summer, oh, my summer,
Oh, my summer's finally here.
There were times I didn't know if
I would make it through the year.

In July, I start relaxing,
Give myself a lot of slack.
Then a letter comes in August . . .
I'm not ready to come back.

Oh, my summer, oh, my summer,
Oh, my summer's finally here.
There were times I didn't know if
I would make it through the year.

© Eric Baylin

Makeup Days

Schools often have to make up days lost due to snow or inclement weather. This extends the calendar year into the summer. Allow casual dress and have a potluck breakfast or lunch on those makeup days so that they'll be more enjoyable.

What Are You Going to Do This Summer?

Make a bulletin board in the staff lounge titled *What Are You Going to Do This Summer?* Ask staff members to bring in pictures of themselves doing their summer activities, and encourage them to be creative in their displays. They can cut pictures from magazines or cartoons and put photographs of their heads on them, or draw themselves doing the activity. They can use photos from a trip or sport.

You could also put up bulletin board paper and have the staff write their name and responses to the questions.

Dee: I am going to sleep for the first month.

Jim: I am going to go on a hiking trip to Colorado.

Sharon: I am taking classes toward my master's degree.

Blast Off to the Summer

Make a rocket ship display with "Blast Off to the Summer" as the heading. As you count down to the end of the school year, have a fun countdown activity.

Variation 1

Have each staff member write his or her name on a rocket-shaped cutout and put it inside the rocket. Draw a name each day to select a winner.

Variation 2

When you make the rocket, make five sections that have opening parts. Behind the openings, place a number. Have staff members draw a number from a hat—this will be their number for the week. Each day, an opening on the rocket will reveal a winning number. The staff member who has the corresponding number is selected as the winner.

Give the winners prizes that they can use over the summer, such as sunblock, a beach towel, or a good book. *(Darlene Roll, Ohio Hi-Point Career Center, Bellefontaine, OH)*

End-of-the-Year Treats

As the end of the year approaches, prepare motivational, appreciative treats for staff members. Put one in their mailbox each day. They will look forward to their daily surprise.

Cheez-It Crackers

Attach the following to a small bag of Cheez-It crackers:

Cheers!	**I**ncredible!
Hallelujah!	**T**errific!
Excellent!	
Exuberation!	
Zuper!	

You are the APPLE of the students' eyes, *juice* because you care!

Apple Juice

Attach to a small bottle of apple juice: "You are the apple of our students' eyes, *juice* because you care!"

Certificate to Perkins Restaurant

Attach the following to the certificate: "Pause the pandemonium! Picky practitioners primarily prefer Perkins (particularly the pastries) to positively pack on pounds prior to partying and playing."

Little Debbie Cake With Nuts

Attach to the cake: "Here is a little something sweet from your good friend, Little Debbie, to help you through the last few *nutty* days of the school year."

Small Package of Oreo Cookies

Attach to the cookies: "Oreo cookies. (Enough said!)"

Small Cup of Pudding

Attach to the pudding: "All of the ♥ you're *pudding* into your work shows in our students' smiles. Thank you!"

Small Package of Pringles Potato Chips

Attach to potato chips: "You have made a big difference this year by *chipping* in as part of our team. Thank you!"

Bite-Sized Snickers Candy Bar

Attach to candy bar and also place small baskets of Snickers in various places around the office:

> Here's a Snickers
>
> There's a Snickers
>
> Everywhere there are Snickers

Small Bottle of Tropicana Orange Juice

Attach to the orange juice:

> Knock, knock.
>
> Who's there?
>
> Orange.
>
> Orange who?
>
> Orange you glad the year is almost over?

Small Neon-Colored Notepads

Attach to the notepads: "We *note*-iced all of your hard work this year. Thanks!" *(Angela Dolheimer, Phineas Davis Elementary School, York, PA)*

What do I want to take home from my summer vacation? *Time.* The wonderful luxury of being at rest. The days when you shut down the mental machinery that keeps life on track and let life simply wander. The days when you stop planning, analyzing, thinking and just are. Summer is my period of grace.

—*Ellen Goodman*

Index

CORWIN
A SAGE Company

The Corwin logo—a raven striding across an open book—represents the union of courage and learning. Corwin is committed to improving education for all learners by publishing books and other professional development resources for those serving the field of PreK–12 education. By providing practical, hands-on materials, Corwin continues to carry out the promise of its motto: **"Helping Educators Do Their Work Better."**